The Importance Of

Rachel Carson

by
Judith Janda Presnall

Lucent Books, P.O. Box 289011, San Diego, CA 92198-9011

These and other titles are included in The Importance Of biography series:

Alexander the Great
Muhammad Ali
Napoleon Bonaparte
Rachel Carson
Cleopatra
Christopher Columbus
Marie Curie
Thomas Edison
Albert Einstein
Benjamin Franklin
Galileo Galilei
Stephen Hawking
Jim Henson
Harry Houdini
Thomas Jefferson
Chief Joseph
Malcolm X
Margaret Mead
Michelangelo
Wolfgang Amadeus Mozart
Sir Isaac Newton
Richard M. Nixon
Louis Pasteur
Jackie Robinson
Anwar Sadat
Margaret Sanger
John Steinbeck
Jim Thorpe
Mark Twain
H.G. Wells

Library of Congress Cataloging-in-Publication Data

Presnall, Judith Janda.
Rachel Carson / by Judith Janda Presnall.
p. cm. — (The Importance of)
Includes bibliographical references (p.) and index.
ISBN 1-56006-052-2 (acid-free paper)
1. Carson, Rachel, 1907-1964—Juvenile literature. 2. Women conservationists—United States—Biography—Juvenile literature. 3. Conservationists—United States—Biography—Juvenile literature. 4. Biologists—United States—Biography—Juvenile literature. [1. Carson, Rachel, 1907-1964. 2. Conservationists. 3. Biologists. 4. Women—Biography.] I. Title. II. Series.
QH31.C33P73 1995
574'.092—dc20
[B]
93-49487
CIP
AC

Printed in the U.S.A.

In loving memory of my mom
Tess M. Janda
who enjoyed flowers, birds, and dogs

Contents

Foreword

THE IMPORTANCE OF biography series deals with individuals who have made a unique contribution to history. The editors of the series have deliberately chosen to cast a wide net and include people from all fields of endeavor. Individuals from politics, music, art, literature, philosophy, science, sports, and religion are all represented. In addition, the editors did not restrict the series to individuals whose accomplishments have helped change the course of history. Of necessity, this criterion would have eliminated many whose contribution was great, though limited. Charles Darwin, for example, was responsible for radically altering the scientific view of the natural history of the world. His achievements continue to impact the study of science today. Others, such as Chief Joseph of the Nez Percé, played a pivotal role in the history of their own people. While Joseph's influence does not extend much beyond the Nez Percé, his nonviolent resistance to white expansion and his continuing role in protecting his tribe and his homeland remain an inspiration to all.

These biographies are more than factual chronicles. Each volume attempts to emphasize an individual's contributions both in his or her own time and for posterity. For example, the voyages of Christopher Columbus opened the way to European colonization of the New World. Unquestionably, his encounter with the New World brought monumental changes to both Europe and the Americas in his day. Today, however, the broader impact of Columbus's voyages is being critically scrutinized. *Christopher Columbus,* as well as every biography in The Importance Of series, includes and evaluates the most recent scholarship available on each subject.

Each author includes a wide variety of primary and secondary source quotations to document and substantiate his or her work. All quotes are footnoted to show readers exactly how and where biographers derive their information, as well as to provide stepping stones to further research. These quotations enliven the text by giving readers eyewitness views of the life and times of each individual covered in The Importance Of series.

Finally, each volume is enhanced by photographs, bibliographies, chronologies, and comprehensive indexes. For both the casual reader and the student engaged in research, The Importance Of biographies will be a fascinating adventure into the lives of people who have helped shape humanity's past and present, and who will continue to shape its future.

Important Dates in the Life of Rachel Carson

- **1907** — Rachel Louise Carson is born on May 27 in Springdale, Pennsylvania.
- **1918** — *St. Nicholas* magazine publishes Carson's story, "A Battle in the Clouds," beginning her writing career.
- **1925-1929** — Attends Pennsylvania College for Women (now Chatham College) in Pittsburgh; receives bachelor's degree in science.
- **1929** — Attends Woods Hole Marine Biological Laboratory on summer fellowship.
- **1929-1932** — Does graduate study at Johns Hopkins University; receives master's degree in marine zoology.
- **1935-1952** — Has career with U.S. Bureau of Fisheries (later Fish & Wildlife Service), including work as radio script writer, junior aquatic biologist, aquatic biologist, assistant to chief, and editor-in-chief.
- **1937** — With help of mother, begins raising nieces Marjorie and Virginia Williams; Carson's article, "Undersea," is published in *Atlantic Monthly*.
- **1941** — First book, *Under the Sea-Wind*, is published.
- **1951** — *The Sea Around Us* is published and makes best-seller list.
- **1955** — *The Edge of the Sea* is published.
- **1957** — Adopts five-year-old grandnephew, Roger Christie.
- **1960** — Carson has breast tumor removed.
- **1962** — *Silent Spring* is published; more than forty bills are passed to regulate pesticides.
- **1963** — Carson appears on *CBS Reports* TV along with a chemist and government officials to defend her views.
- **1964** — April 14, Rachel Carson dies of cancer and heart disease.
- **1965** — Her final book, *The Sense of Wonder*, is published posthumously.
- **1980** — Presidential Medal of Freedom is awarded posthumously to Carson by President Jimmy Carter.

Defending Nature's Creatures

The name Rachel Carson is linked to her powerful book, *Silent Spring*, which alerted an uninformed public about dangerous chemicals that were being sprayed heavily everywhere—over forests, farms, neighborhoods, and even school playgrounds. *Silent Spring* aroused the world and changed the public's attitude toward the environment forever.

In the early 1900s when Rachel Carson was growing up, the land seemed vast and people weren't aware that they could harm it. Air, land, and water pollution were not concerns of the world. No environmental regulations were in place. Chemical companies were unrestricted in their zeal to provide more and better pesticides to fight destructive, annoying, and disease-carrying insects. Having confidence in technology, people believed that chemicals could solve nature's pest problems. People were ignorant of the damage done by sprayed poisons seeping into the earth and into waterways.

By the late 1950s the United States was producing nearly five hundred new chemicals annually. This abundance had an overwhelmingly negative effect on nature. Between 1947 and 1960, production of synthetic pesticides in the United States increased fivefold. The use of pesticides became a worldwide problem. The chemicals had been so thoroughly distributed that they could be found virtually every-

A man sprays malathion to eradicate Mediterranean fruit flies. Rachel Carson proposed using natural methods, such as releasing sterile flies in residential neighborhoods.

where: in rivers, groundwater, and soil; in fish, birds, reptiles, animals, and even humans. These chemicals were strong enough to have toxic effects on the food chain, eventually affecting plants and animals eaten by humans. The broad general sprayings caused the destruction of beneficial species and resulted in an unbalanced ecosystem. DDT also brought on an "age of resistance" in insects, with the result that stronger chemicals were required to kill the more vigorous strains.

Carson's goal in writing *Silent Spring* was to educate the public as well as to reach people in authority. Within two weeks, *Silent Spring* made the *New York Times* best-seller list and eventually sold 500,000 copies.

With the publication of *Silent Spring*, people all over the world became aware of problems that had been kept secret. The book shocked and angered readers. Scientists did not understand how important it was for our species to be in harmony with nature. They thought they could alter ecosystems without producing negative long-term effects. Carson's research proved them wrong.

Silent Spring did not use scientific jargon; it told the public in simple words that our environment was in trouble. The book brought about positive action everywhere. Town meetings, newspaper articles, letters to Congress, and federal legislation all reflected the public's growing environmental concern.

Rachel Carson was a woman who had two loves: nature and writing. Using her reputation as a best-selling author of books about the sea, she combined her writing skills with her university degrees in biology and zoology to publicize the environmental horrors she saw in the United States and other parts of the world. The distinguished nonfiction writer took on the project herself because no one else suitable or willing could be found. The introduction to the public of the controversial subject would create havoc. The pesticide industry was outraged and tried to discredit Carson's findings. Her courageous protest in *Silent Spring* defended the natural world and created a worldwide environmental revolution. She has been called the founder of today's ecology movement. The greatest tribute to Rachel Carson is reflected in the vast number of people who are now working to save our environment.

In 1962 Rachel Carson informed the world of the dangers of pesticides in her book Silent Spring.

Rachel Carson was a biologist, not a crusader. But because of her ability to combine authoritative knowledge with clear, understandable, and beautiful language, she became one of the most influential women of our time.

Chapter

1 Rural Heaven

Rachel Louise Carson was born on May 27, 1907, in a small two-story wooden house that had no plumbing, no furnace, and no electricity. The four-room house, located in the town of Springdale along Pennsylvania's Allegheny River, was surrounded by acres of woods. The kitchen was a lean-to shed attached to the back of the house. The refrigerator was a tiny outdoor building with a spring running through it. This "springhouse" was a source for water and also kept food cool. Birds flitted in the trees, crickets filled the fields with their music, bees pollinated the blossoms, fish swam in the river's icy waters, and opossum, quail, rabbits, and other creatures shared the property.

The household included Rachel's parents, Robert Warden Carson and Maria Frazier McLean Carson; a ten-year-old sister, Marian; and an eight-year-old brother, Robert Jr.

Rachel's father had bought the house and sixty-five acres of heavily wooded farmland before Rachel was born, in the belief that the population of twelve hundred people would grow rapidly because the little town was only fifteen miles north of the booming steel city of Pittsburgh. He hoped to get rich by selling off small portions of the family's land to build homes. Unfortunately, the plan failed. Thus, instead of becoming rich, Robert Carson worked in a Pittsburgh power plant and also sold insurance for a few years. Although educated and articulate, Carson had a reserved personality and made few local friends. In their home Rachel's mother taught piano for fifty cents a lesson to help the family's finances.

Rachel is pictured on her mother's lap flanked by her sister, Marian, and her brother, Robert.

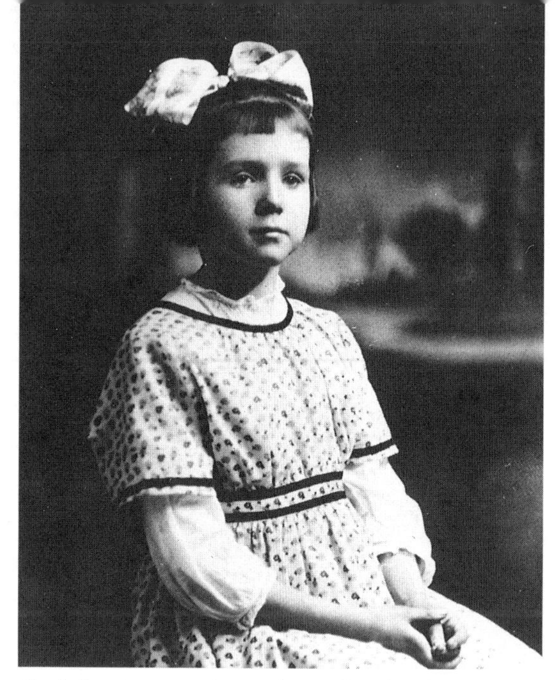

Rachel, age seven, is wearing a Sunday dress that her mother made.

The farm supplied the Carsons with food. They owned a few cows for milk, chickens for eggs, a horse to pull their wagon and carriage, and pigs for meat. Rachel and her brother and sister did the usual farm chores of feeding the animals, gathering eggs, and churning milk into butter and cheese. They also helped with the vegetable gardens, where the Carsons grew much of their food. To bring in additional money, the family sold pippin, russet, Rome Beauties, and other varieties of apples from their ten-acre orchard.

The Carsons had been told that their farmland probably had coal underneath it, which they could sell to a mining company. But even though the family needed the money, Robert Carson would not allow the beautiful land to be disfigured with huge holes.

A Strong Mother-Daughter Bond

The most inspirational person in Rachel's life was her mother. Maria Carson, a former teacher, had graduated from Pennsylvania's Washington Seminary for Women. One biographer, Marty Jezer, describes Rachel's mother as follows:

The Carsons' home in Springdale, Pennsylvania. Rachel enjoyed exploring the nearby rivers, fields, and ponds.

A woman of great personal integrity, Maria Carson had a tremendous influence on her daughter's life. After her father died when she was eleven, Maria had been raised in a household of women in Washington, Pennsylvania. She grew into a confident, self-reliant young woman and became a teacher, largely because it was one of the few career opportunities open to middle-class women at the time.[1]

Rachel shares her love of books with her dog, Candy, on their rural Pennsylvania farm.

Maria Carson had a special fondness for nature, and that characteristic led to the formation of a strong bond between mother and daughter. "Those interests, I know, I inherited from my mother and have always shared with her,"[2] Rachel had said.

Taking a picnic lunch, Rachel and her mother explored their rural farm and woods regularly. The young girl chased butterflies and peeked at bird eggs. Rachel was fascinated with everything she saw and asked many questions. Her mother taught her the names of insects, birds, and plants. The rivers, fields, and ponds were like a classroom to Rachel. Whenever her mother couldn't answer the child's questions, they would search together for the answers in books.

Sometimes her mother woke Rachel early in the morning to hear the singing birds. On summer evenings they sat on the darkened porch to watch fireflies signal mating codes and listen to crickets and frogs chirp and croak their songs to each other.

"I can remember no time when I wasn't interested in the out-of-doors and the whole world of nature,"[3] Rachel said many years later.

Rachel was a shy child and, like her father, didn't make friends easily. Because the family lived in an isolated area, she had few playmates. Yet Rachel wasn't lonely or bored. She was busy with her pets, exploring the woods, or reading books. Besides several cats, Rachel had a dog, Candy, who was her loyal companion.

"I was rather a solitary child and spent a great deal of time in woods and beside streams, learning the birds and the insects and flowers,"[4] reported Rachel.

Rachel's World

Without television, transistor radios, or movies, the Carson family made their own entertainment. They spent many evenings enjoying music and literature. After dinner they sang while Maria played the piano. On other nights they read to each other while crunching on apples from their orchard.

When Rachel was young, she took great joy in reading Beatrix Potter's books with animal characters such as Peter Rabbit, a cat named Tabitha Twitchet, and a

The Little Brown House.
Once upon a time, two little wrens were hunting a little house to set up housekeeping. All at once they saw a dear little brown house with a green roof. "Now that is just what we need," said Mr Wren to Jenny.

Already showing her concern for nature in the second grade, Rachel wrote "The Little Brown House."

dog, Pickles. In fact, all animal stories appealed to her. Later, Rachel began reading about real-life animals.

As a child she decided that someday she would write books. In an interview later in life, Rachel said:

> I have no idea why. There were no writers in the family. I read a great deal almost from infancy [her mother had read out loud to her] and I suppose I must have realized someone wrote the books and thought it would be fun to make up stories, too.[5]

Because Marian and young Robert were ten and eight years older, they spent little time with Rachel. Sometimes Marian would practice dancing to popular music in the parlor as Rachel watched. Robert Junior tinkered with tools and wires, building small projects, and took Rachel hunting a few times. Rachel found hunting with her brother a painful experience. Even though the family used the wild rabbits Robert killed for food, as they did with other barnyard animals, Rachel didn't like to watch the shooting. Finally she worked up enough courage to tell her brother about her feelings; and Robert gave up hunting.

Rachel as a Student

At age six Rachel began attending School Street School in Springdale. She walked to school, about half a mile away. Rachel loved learning, but she attended school very irregularly. Because Rachel had had scarlet fever as a young child, Maria was afraid the girl might catch one of the other childhood diseases, such as diphtheria, whooping cough, measles, or typhoid fever. She often kept Rachel home from school when other children had colds or when the snow drifts were too high to walk through.

On days when Rachel missed school, her mother taught her at home and made sure she was current with what her classmates were learning.

> We used to say her mother did all her homework for her [one girl recalled in later years]. We knew it wasn't true, of

course. When Rachel was called on to recite in class, she was always prepared. She didn't flounder. What Mrs. Carson did was harder and perfectly fair. She tutored Rachel, so that her absences didn't make much difference.[6]

Because of her many absences, Rachel did not form close friendships at school.

When Rachel was in the second grade, she made up rhyming poems, like "a frog on a log" and "a mouse in a house." She wrote her poems in a booklet, drew pictures of animals and birds to accompany them, and gave the booklet to her father. The family's happiness with her project encouraged Rachel to continue writing.

When Rachel was ten, Marian married and Robert Junior joined the U.S. Army Aviation Service, the forerunner of today's Air Force. Now Rachel was the only child at home. She used her lonely hours to write stories. In 1917, when World War I was being fought in Europe, Robert wrote home telling the family what was going on overseas. In one of his letters, he told about a brave aviator whose plane was about to crash after being hit over Germany. The pilot crawled out onto the wing to balance the plane. The Germans were so impressed with the pilot's skill, they let him land safely.

Becoming a Writer

This story fascinated Rachel so much that she wrote it up, titled it "A Battle in the Clouds," and mailed it to a children's magazine, *St. Nicholas,* for their special "St. Nicholas League" section for young readers' contributions. Many months later, in the September 1918 issue, the story was published.

The magazine awarded Rachel second prize, the Silver Badge, and ten dollars. Later in life, Rachel remarked:

> I doubt that any royalty check of recent years has given me as great joy as the notice of the award. . . . Perhaps that early experience of seeing my work in print played its part in fostering my childhood dream of becoming a writer.[7]

But that was just the beginning. Two more of Rachel's stories were published in *St. Nicholas* magazine. One, "A Message to the Front," in February 1919, won her the Gold Badge award. A third story, "A Famous Sea-Fight," printed in August 1919, made her an "Honor Member." *St. Nicholas* had now published three stories by Rachel in twelve months. The ecstasy Rachel felt confirmed what she was going to be—a writer.

For an English class assignment, Rachel wrote an essay about *St. Nicholas* magazine. The magazine's advertising department paid her a penny per word, a little over three dollars, for the essay. This was Rachel's first nonprize payment. At age eleven Rachel took pride in saying that she was now a "professional writer."

The School Street School ended at the tenth grade. Rachel attended Parnassus Senior High School in New Kensington for her junior and senior years. The school was about three miles from home across the Allegheny River, and Rachel rode a streetcar to get there. In high school Rachel earned straight A's. Her classmates respected her and recognized her determination for success. Next to her senior photo in the yearbook were the following lines:

A Battle in the Clouds
By Rachel L. Carson (Age 10)

The September 1918 issue of St. Nicholas *magazine published Rachel's first submission, earning her an award and a small cash prize. This excerpt of the story is taken from Philip Sterling's biography,* Sea and Earth: The Life of Rachel Carson.

"This is a story about a famous aviator [pilot], who was in the Royal Flying Corps until he was killed in this country [the United States] instructing other men. The main facts of this story were told to me by my brother, who is a soldier. The aviator had been several years in France. One day, when he and one of his companions were flying, a German plane suddenly burst upon them from behind a cloud. The two planes began firing, and the anti-aircraft guns of the Allies and Germans began firing. For a while, neither plane was injured, but soon . . . a part of one wing of the Canadian aviator's plane had been shot away. The plane wavered, and [the pilot] knew that if something was not done promptly, the plane would fall. He saw there was only one thing to do, and he did it quickly. He crawled out along the wing, inch by inch, until he reached the end. He then hung from the end of the wing, his weight making the plane balance properly. The Germans saw him but could not but respect and admire the daring and courage of the aviator, and did not fire until the plane landed safely. The aviator was killed a few months ago in a training camp in this country, and, in my opinion, the Allies, by his death, lost a brave and daring soldier."

Rachel's like the mid-day sun
Always very bright.
Never stops her studying
'Til she gets it right.[8]

Because of her excellent grades, Rachel was awarded a hundred-dollar scholarship to the Pennsylvania College for Women [known as Chatham College since 1955] in Pittsburgh. The small campus, which was close to her home, had high academic standards, and offered scholarships, was perfect for Rachel.

If it hadn't been for the scholarship and other unofficial aid from private sources (arranged for by the college president, Cora Helen Coolidge), Rachel's family could not have afforded the thousand-dollar yearly tuition and expenses. Choosing English literature as her main course of study, Rachel was eager to fulfill her dreams of becoming a writer.

Chapter

2 College Years Lure Rachel to Nature

When Rachel entered Pennsylvania College for Women in 1925, it was a picturesque campus of ivy-covered buildings, flowing lawns, and lush woods. Most of the three hundred students came from wealthy families and had expensive wardrobes. Rachel couldn't afford stylish outfits, but she didn't care. Her goal was to get good grades and learn as much as possible.

Rachel's college classmates called her the commuter student, since every weekend either Rachel went home or her mother came to the campus.

Her classmates wondered about the student who spent so much time studying and writing in the library. One woman later said of Rachel:

> She wasn't anti-social. She just wasn't social. Being poor had some bearing on that. She didn't have the clothes or the extra things a girl needed at college then. And Rachel did have to accept financial help, which was more of a stigma in those days than later.[9]

Another classmate, Mary Kolb, remembered:

> Though she was much more of a scholar than the rest of us and in a way withdrawn, she entered into things with great spirit. When you asked her to do something, she did it wholeheartedly—if she wanted to do it.[10]

English and Writing—A Priority

Since her main interest was to be a writer, English was Rachel's favorite subject. An English professor, Grace Croff, recognized Rachel's talent with words early on. In later years, Rachel would remember Grace Croff as "a wonderful woman who gave [taught] my course in English composition and really exerted quite an influence on my life."[11]

Rachel used her writing skills as a reporter on the student paper, *The Arrow*. The student paper had a special literary supplement, *Englicode*, which published Rachel's short story "The Master of the Ship's Light." This story described what she had imagined the sea to be:

> The coast was less hospitable than the people who inhabited it. Over the surface of the long lazy swells that rolled in on the shallow beach, played dark formless shadows or patches of white foam, betraying the menacing reefs

> beneath. When the icy winds swept down from the Straits, towering waves beat upon the coast with uncontrollable fury, and the booming of the breakers resounded for miles.[12]

Rachel also wrote poetry and submitted many of her poems to magazines. Biographer Paul Brooks reports Carson's early failures as an unpublished poet:

> Judging from the large and varied collection of rejection slips preserved in her files, Rachel Carson first sought publication as a poet. Beginning not later than her senior year in college, and probably before (most of the form rejections are undated), she submitted verse to *Poetry, The Atlantic Monthly, Good Housekeeping, Woman's Home Companion, The Saturday Evening Post, Century Magazine, American Magazine, The Delineator, The Youth's Companion,* and several other periodicals which—like many on this list—live only in fading memory. She was persistent, but apparently wholly unsuccessful.[13]

Science Classes Pull at Rachel's Heart

Since students were required to take at least two semesters of science, Rachel enrolled in Biology 1 and 2 in her sophomore year. Expecting the class to consist of dull definitions and tiring lab experiments, Rachel was astonished by the enthusiasm and fast pace of Mary Scott Skinker. This biology teacher made the subject fascinating. Miss Skinker taught her students to understand the web of life and how every living thing from a tiny protozoan to a huge whale fits in. Rachel stated that "my childhood interest in natural history found a new and clearer focus in the biological sciences."[14]

Rachel had two good friends in her sophomore biology class: Mary Frye and Dorothy Thompson. Both these young women shared Rachel's enthusiasm for science, and their friendships continued after college.

Rachel visits with her college English professor, Grace Croff.

Does Rachel Have a Cat's Personality?

While in college, Rachel wrote a story, "Why I Am a Pessimist," using the voice of a cat, for a campus publication, the Englicode. *This excerpt appears in Philip Sterling's biography* Sea and Earth.

"No one in this household pays any attention to me. Not that I can't get along without them well enough but it's the principle of the thing. . . .The family keeps bothering me about little details that don't matter. If I'm not good enough to talk to and associate with, I'm not good enough for them to torment, either. . . .They just don't get my viewpoint. . . . Some day I'm going away to live with a nice old lady who hasn't any other cats. She'll believe in a cat's right to be independent, and as good as anyone else. Then won't I come back here at night and howl on the fence! Won't I though!"

A Contrary Decision

When Rachel returned for her junior year at Pennsylvania College for Women, she decided to switch her major from English to science. The decision bothered her professors, her classmates, and even the college president. Rachel's interest in biology had deepened, however, and for her junior and senior years she signed up for classes in embryology and genetics, bacteriology, histology [study of tissues], and chemistry. Besides all the science courses, Rachel had two years of French, and one year each of German and Italian.

Since Rachel was considered to be Grace Croff's star student, Croff was saddened by Rachel's change in major. The English professor had had high literary hopes for Rachel. Classmates, too, felt that Rachel was making a mistake because she would have to take additional classes. But Rachel welcomed the new challenge and

Carson graduated from the Pennsylvania College for Women in 1929. A scholarship enabled her to attend graduate school at Johns Hopkins University.

did not mind the many laboratory hours that were required.

The college president, Miss Coolidge, who took great pride in Rachel's literary talent, worried about whether a woman could succeed in the field of science. In the 1920s very few scientists were women; Miss Coolidge did not think that being a science instructor was as prestigious as being a talented writer.

A Mentor and Friend

Mary Skinker, the biology instructor, was delighted by Rachel's decision. On field trips to Cook State Forest, McConnell's Mill, and other rural locations, Rachel made many discoveries. She identified wild flowers and various birds, admired undamaged wildernesses, and even uncovered a fish fossil. Miss Skinker became Rachel's mentor and good friend.

In a letter to her friend Mary Frye, who was in Florida recovering from an illness, Rachel wrote:

> We can have a great time in some of those courses. Yesterday we had lots of fun dissecting *Amphioxus* [small, boneless, fishlike animals]. We're going to do the dog-fish next week. . . . The dog-fish is such fun. I wish we were doing it together. They make your hands and books and everything smell awful, though. . . . Do bring back a Portuguese Man of War [large, floating, tubelike warm-sea animal].[15]

During Rachel's senior year, Mary Skinker took a leave of absence to pursue her Ph.D. at Johns Hopkins University. Rachel missed her favorite instructor's support and enthusiasm. The campus felt empty, but the two women kept in touch by exchanging letters.

Rachel was active in college activities. She was a member of the literary club

Reactions to Rachel's Changing Her College Major

A letter excerpted from Sea and Earth, *Philip Sterling's biography, shows the reactions to Rachel's decision to change her major from English to biology. Rachel wrote to Mary Frye, her biology lab friend:*

"I have something very exciting to tell you. I've changed my major. To what? Biology, of course! All year I've been enjoying the people who were majoring in it. I finally decided to do it. [The college president] Miss Coolidge, etc., have been kicking up a fine row about my schedule and my major in general. . . . You ought to see the reactions I get. I've gotten bawled out and called all sorts of blankety-blank names so much that it's beginning to get monotonous. That's all from the other girls, of course."

Rachel (top row, second from right) was goalkeeper on her college field hockey team.

Omega. In addition, with Mary Frye and Dorothy Thompson, she organized a science club, naming it Mu Sigma, using Mary Skinker's initials M.S. from the Greek alphabet (MΣ). The members elected Rachel as the club's first president. Rachel continued her work on the college newspaper and also played campus sports. A classmate, Margaret Wooldridge, recalled:

> Rachel was a perennial substitute on the intramural hockey, baseball, and basketball teams. She was eligible because she attended enough practice sessions, but those first two years she wasn't quite good enough to make a regular place on the team.[16]

However, Rachel became quite good at field hockey in her junior and senior years and as a goalkeeper helped her team to win intramural championship games in 1928 and 1929.

In her senior year, Rachel was copy editor of *The Arrow.* This assignment was ideal for Rachel, who was a perfectionist. It allowed her to fix other students' writing by correcting spelling and punctuation, and by choosing the perfect words to make the stories better.

Benefits for the Scholarly Student

In her final months at college in 1929, Rachel had good news. Besides graduating magna cum laude [with high honors], with a major in biology and a minor in English, she received from Johns Hopkins University in Baltimore a $200 scholarship for graduate study. Recommendations by the Pennsylvania College for Women also led to a summer fellowship [graduate student support money], which allowed Rachel to study at the Marine Biological Laboratory at Woods Hole, located on the southwestern tip of Cape Cod in Massachusetts. Rachel was thrilled to be going to this famous marine research center and working within the scientific community of people who had authored many of the

A center for ocean research, the Woods Hole Marine Biological Laboratory in Massachusetts became a favorite study place for Carson. The summer of college graduation, Rachel spent six weeks there on a scholarship.

books and articles she had read. At last, Rachel would fulfill her dream of being near the ocean:

> As a very small child I was fascinated by the ocean, although I had never seen it. I dreamed of it and longed to see it, and I read all the sea literature I could find.[17]

In July Rachel left by train for her exciting trip to Woods Hole and her very first visit to the sea. She first stopped in Baltimore to meet her adviser, Dr. R.P. Cowles, of the zoology department at Johns Hopkins. Next, Rachel visited her former biology teacher, Mary Skinker, who was living in Washington, D.C. About a week later Rachel toured New York City for a day. Then she left on a passenger boat for the trip to Woods Hole. Despite a pelting rain, Rachel remained on the outside deck. She loved breathing the salty air, and not being able to see land gave her a feeling of solitude. In the morning she arrived at her destination.

For the next six weeks at Woods Hole, Rachel lived in a rented room with her former lab partner Mary Frye, who was also there on a scholarship. The windy village, with research ships anchored at docks, the Marine Biological Laboratory, the tide pools, the aquarium, and the beaches, enabled Rachel to study many live sea creatures. Rachel enjoyed firsthand involvement with fish, squid, starfish, sea anemones, and scallops. Sometimes she was emotional in her discoveries:

> I stood knee-deep in that racing water, and at the time could barely see those darting, silver bits of life [mullet fish] for my tears.[18]

Her research project at Woods Hole was to study and write a paper on the cranial nerves of turtles and the terminal nerves in lizards and snakes. With the latest laboratory equipment, an excellent library, oceanographic scientists all around her, plus the Atlantic Ocean, Rachel was in heaven. She also had time to get a tan and practice her swimming skills. Even though there were few women scientists at Woods Hole, Rachel felt she fit in with this community of people. The summer experience convinced Rachel that a career in marine studies was the correct choice. She was energized and ready to begin her studies at Johns Hopkins.

Chapter

3 The Magic of the Seas

After completing her summer session at Woods Hole in 1929, Carson traveled to Washington, D.C., to call on Elmer Higgins, head of the U.S. Bureau of Fisheries, Scientific Inquiry Division. Carson entered the bureaucrat's office and said, "I have a Bachelor of Arts degree and will begin to work for my Master's degree in marine biology next month. I think I'd like to work in the fishery research field and I'd be grateful for any advice you can give me."[19]

The two talked for an hour. Carson asked many questions. For example, she wanted to know what opportunities were open for women as marine scientists, what type of work was done at the Bureau of Fisheries, and what courses she should

Rachel worked on her master's degree in marine biology at Johns Hopkins University during the Great Depression. To help with expenses, Rachel worked as a teaching and lab assistant at JHU from 1929 to 1932.

choose at Johns Hopkins to qualify as a working marine biologist. Higgins said that there was open prejudice against women biologists, especially for jobs in industry and in museums. The only scientific jobs readily open to women were teaching and government work. This information did not discourage Carson.

Prosperity Changes to Gloom

At Johns Hopkins, Carson immersed herself in graduate studies. The outside world and its problems seemed distant for a while. Since the end of World War I in 1919, the country had been enjoying prosperity. High wages, more products, increased buying, plus investing in speculative [risky] stock ventures became common. In October 1929, however, the feverish buying of stocks exhausted itself and frantic selling took place. Prices dropped dramatically, and thousands of people lost all they had invested. The business of the New York Stock Exchange collapsed.

Thus began the years of the Great Depression. Hundreds of banks failed, hundreds of factories and mills closed, and unemployment rose drastically. At one point nearly one-third of the job force was out of work.

The stock market crash happened just two months after Carson had started her graduate studies. Many Americans had to put their dreams on hold, and Rachel's family was no exception. Since no one could afford to buy real estate, Rachel persuaded her parents to abandon their Springdale, Pennsylvania, property in January 1930 and come to live with her. Rachel had rented a cottage thirteen miles from Baltimore; the small country home was a thirty-minute trolley ride to Johns Hopkins.

For a time in 1931, Rachel's brother Robert also came to live in the house outside Baltimore. His business in Pittsburgh was not making money, a common occurrence during the depression, and he became a radio-repairs estimator. One evening Robert returned from work with a Persian cat: a customer who couldn't pay had exchanged Mitzi, a pedigreed female, for Rachel's brother's services. Trading goods and services was common in those days because money was scarce. Mitzi was a welcome guest, since both Rachel and her mother were fond of cats. Mitzi and her kittens were special members of the Carson household for many years.

A portrait of Rachel taken while she was a student at Johns Hopkins University.

A Glowing Recommendation

Sea and Earth, Philip Sterling's biography of Rachel Carson, contains this letter from Dr. Cowles, Rachel's adviser at Johns Hopkins University, which helped Carson obtain a teaching job at the University of Maryland.

"It is a pleasure for me to recommend to you Miss Rachel Carson who is applying for a position as half-time assistant in zoology at the University of Maryland. Miss Carson is a young lady of excellent character. She is pleasing in appearance and capable in everything that she does. Her scholarship has been high in her undergraduate studies and also in her graduate work here. . . . The students, both male and female, like and respect her, and Miss Grace Lippy, under whom she was assisting (in summer school), speaks very highly of her. I recommend Miss Carson to you without question."

Earning While Learning

Fortunately, Carson was able to remain in school for the next three years, in spite of the depression. During these busy years of graduate study, she earned money as a teaching assistant in biology at the Johns Hopkins summer school.

In a letter to her friend Dorothy Thompson, Carson wrote:

> I've just put in a tough day at the lab. Getting the lab ready for 45 students is no fun. I have to do everything myself. A lot of glassware needs washing, and I have to see to it that each table is supplied with a long list of apparatus. I have most of my lab material collected and I've learned a lot about the how and where of such things. I met Miss Lippy, my "boss" today, and she seems to be a very likable sort of person, and I think will be very easy to work with.[20]

Miss Lippy liked Carson so well that she rehired her for each summer session for the next six years.

In her second year of graduate work Carson worked part-time as a lab assistant to Dr. Raymond Pearl, who was a geneticist, a biologist who studies heredity. For two summers Carson also worked on research projects for several weeks at Woods Hole, linking herself closely to her beloved sea.

Since Carson had to spend part of her time earning money, she could not be a full-time student. She began her third year in the fall of 1931, again searching for work. Carson's adviser, Dr. Cowles, came to her rescue with a note of recommendation to Professor C.J. Pierson at the University of Maryland in College Park. Carson was happy to get a part-time job as a teaching assistant. She made the seventy-mile round trip to College Park by bus several times a week.

When Carson began her studies at Johns Hopkins, she was determined to do well. Her classes and laboratory periods added up to a forty-six-hour week. Her day began at 7 A.M., and she spent most evenings in the lab.

Finding a suitable master's thesis project was a top priority. After a series of disappointing results in the first year with embryos of turtles, snakes, lizards, and squirrels, Carson and Dr. Cowles decided on a project: she would study the development of the pronephros of the channel catfish. The pronephros is the catfish's temporary kidney, which appears in the egg and disappears on the eleventh day, when the animal becomes a free-swimming larva.

Carson's project required hundreds of hours at the microscope, where she examined thin slices of catfish egg and larva. She also had to read about catfish physiology, or the functions and processes of its vital organs. Carson read thousands of

The microscope allowed Rachel to observe tide-pool specimens up close.

Rachel's Relationship with Men

In her biography Rachel Carson, *Carol B. Gartner describes Carson's dating life.*

"There is little evidence of male friends during Carson's college years. In letters from that period, she mentions only one big date, for her junior prom. References to men in letters written while she was in graduate school merely describe competition in laboratory work. Her comment to an interviewer that she never married 'because I didn't have time' is often quoted, but there is no reason to believe that she ever wanted to marry, even though she wrote sympathetically to a college friend about the difficulties of marrying during the depression."

Rachel enjoys writing while savoring the ocean at Woods Hole. The Cape Cod area blends sea breezes with sunlit sparkling water and floating seagulls.

pages, not only in English but also in French, German, and Italian.

When not working, Carson devoted the rest of her time to her thesis, which required many hours of lab work, 60 drawings, 8 microphotographs [enlargements of pinpoint-sized organisms], and 108 manuscript pages. The project was entitled "The Development of the Pronephros During the Embryonic and Early Larval Life of the Catfish (*Ictalurus punctatus*)."

Carson received her master's degree in marine zoology from Johns Hopkins University in June 1932. Still unable to make regular payments on a $1,600 college tuition debt to Pennsylvania College for Women, Carson gave the college permission to sell her Springdale real estate (a gift from her father), which the school was holding in trust.

The country was still in the depression and jobs were scarce, especially for a new graduate in marine zoology. For several years, Carson continued teaching biology part-time both at the University of Maryland and at Johns Hopkins summer sessions, hoping to find more permanent work.

New Responsibilities

In July 1935, Rachel's father died of a heart attack. In a state of shock and grief, Rachel, at age twenty-eight, needed to support her mother as well as herself. With this new responsibility, Rachel looked for another job to supplement her teaching income.

Carson decided to revisit Elmer Higgins at the U.S. Bureau of Fisheries in Washington, from whom she had asked advice just before beginning her graduate courses six years ago. It turned out that Higgins remembered Carson, and as luck would have it, she appeared at just the right time.

The Bureau of Fisheries had been assigned to do weekly radio broadcasts about fishery and marine life, presented as *Romance Under the Waters*. The professional radio writer who was hired knew nothing about marine biology and had quickly run out of ideas. Carson recalled the incident:

> I happened in one morning when the chief of the biology division [Elmer Higgins] was feeling rather desperate—I think at that point he was having to write the scripts himself. He

talked to me a few minutes and then said: "I've never seen a written word of yours, but I'm going to take a sporting chance." That little job, which eventually led to a permanent appointment as a biologist, was in its way, a turning point.[21]

Carson was paid $1,000 for fifty-two scripts, nicknamed "Seven-Minute Fish Tales." The fascinating tales told about ocean dwellers and promoted the bureau's work of conserving ocean resources and regulating fish harvests. Although the at-home job was only part-time and temporary, Carson was happy to do it. The scripts were later revised and put into a brochure issued by the Government Printing Office. At last Rachel was able to combine her two loves: writing and science.

When an opening for a junior aquatic biologist was announced, Carson took the federal civil service examination. Carson, the only woman taking the test, scored the highest and was hired as a permanent civil service employee at a yearly salary of $2,000 in August 1936. Finally, Rachel and her mother had some financial security.

Elmer Higgins requested that Carson work in his department, where she researched public inquiries and translated scientific information into simple language.

A Growing Family

To be closer to the Washington bureau, Rachel and her mother moved to Silver Spring, Maryland. While Rachel worked, Maria Carson cooked, cleaned, and shopped. Since Rachel hated cooking, the arrangement was completely satisfactory.

The following year, in 1937, Rachel's forty-year-old sister, Marian Williams, died of pneumonia. Rachel and her mother chose to raise Marian's two daughters, since Marian had been divorced, and the girls' father wasn't a part of their lives. Marjorie and Virginia Williams were in elemen-

Carson's Love of Beautiful Words Makes Her a Slow Writer

In The House of Life: Rachel Carson at Work, *biographer and editor Paul Brooks quotes Carson and describes her method of composing manuscripts for publication.*

"On a 'very good day,' she might do fifteen hundred words; the average was nearer five hundred. 'I am a slow writer, enjoying the stimulating pursuit of research far more than the drudgery of turning out manuscript . . .' [she said]. Her first drafts were generally in longhand; she would revise and revise until she was satisfied with the result, which always had to pass the final test of being read aloud to her, as she listened 'for passages where disharmonies of sound might distract attention from the thought.'"

At home, Rachel types manuscripts from her longhand notes. She published "Undersea" in the distinguished Atlantic Monthly *magazine.*

tary school. Rachel now supported herself and three other people. Grandmother Maria and Aunt Rachel kept laughter and fun in the home, however, introducing the young girls to the animals of the woods and marshes. Later Virginia recalled life in Silver Spring: "Rachel was more like an older sister; she was a lot of fun, and certainly made a happy home for us."[22]

Extra money came from Carson's writing skills. She began to use her knowledge of the sea and nature to write articles for the *Baltimore Sunday Sun*, a local paper, earning ten to twenty dollars for each article. Carson wrote at home late in the evening when the house was quiet. She wrote in longhand and her mother helped by typing the projects.

As one assignment, Elmer Higgins had asked Carson to write an introduction for the government brochure based on her "fish tale" radio scripts. The introduction was supposed to string all the sea animal stories together. Carson felt the task was simple enough, and she produced an essay explaining about life beneath the surface of the ocean, describing sea creatures of all shapes and sizes, in beautiful literary words.

Carson had worked diligently on the essay and was disappointed when Higgins didn't want to use it. "I don't think it will do. Better try again. But send this one to the *Atlantic*,"[23] he said. The *Atlantic Monthly* was a prestigious magazine that had published such distinguished authors as Emerson and Thoreau. Carson, feeling that an unknown author would not arouse interest there, put her manuscript in a drawer.

How About Citizenship Papers for the European Starling?

In 1939 Carson wrote an essay for Nature *about the advantages of the starling, a bird originally imported from Europe that had earned the respect of farmers by gobbling and feeding to its young a great many destructive insects each day.*

"There is good reason to suppose that every one of the uncounted millions of starlings now inhabiting the United States traces lineage to two colonies of birds imported from Europe and liberated in New York's Central Park in the springs of 1890 and 1891. . . . In spite of his remarkable success as a pioneer, the starling probably has fewer friends than almost any other creature that wears feathers. That fact, however, seems to be of very little importance to this cheerful bird with glossy plumage and stumpy tail. Without seeming to care whether the benefiting farmer thanks him or reviles him, he hurries with jerky steps about the farms and gardens in the summer time, carrying more than 100 loads of destructive insects per day to his screaming offspring, cramming his own stomach full of such food as Japanese beetles, caterpillars, and cutworms. . . . The Department of Agriculture pronounced the starling 'one of the most effective bird enemies of terrestrial insect pests in this country.'"

The starling gulps hundreds of pesky insects each day.

New Horizons

A few months later when money was short, Carson took her boss's advice and sent a revised article, "Undersea," to the *Atlantic Monthly*. To her surprise, the magazine paid $75 for the article and published it in the September 1937 issue.

Fan letters began to flow in to Carson, complimenting her on her lively writing about the mysterious underwater world. The *Atlantic*'s "Contributors Column" contained this comment:

> Ever since Jules Verne's imagination went twenty thousand leagues deep, people have wondered what it would

be like to walk on the ocean's floor. Rachel L. Carson . . . has a clear and accurate idea.[24]

"Undersea" also impressed two important people. One was Hendrik Willem van Loon, the successful historian and author of *The Story of Mankind*, then in its forty-ninth printing. Van Loon was so impressed by the article that he contacted his New York publisher, Simon & Schuster. Both the editor-in-chief, Quincy Howe, and Van Loon himself wrote to Carson asking her for ideas about expanding the article into a book. From that *Atlantic* essay, Carson said "everything else followed."[25]

In January 1938, Carson traveled to Old Greenwich, Connecticut, for a meeting with Howe and Van Loon. There, in the home of Van Loon and his wife, Carson discussed her idea to describe the beauty, mystery, and terror of the sea. Using the sea as the main character, Carson would put the reader at the scene of life, with sea creatures and sea birds in supporting roles. She would write about the sea bottom, the open sea, and shore life. The publisher and the famous author were enthusiastic and told her to begin at once. Carson had to write a detailed book outline and several chapters before Simon & Schuster would give her a contract, however.

Writing a Book

Carson wanted the manuscript, entitled *Under the Sea-Wind*, to be scientifically

In her article "Undersea," Carson tried to bring the reader into the ocean—to experience what life was like in the depths of the sea.

correct in every respect. She also wanted to report her thoughts and findings with the most perfectly chosen words, which required many rewrites. Working eight-hour days at the Bureau of Fisheries, though, she had only weekends and evenings to research and write the book.

Finally, after six months, she had completed the outline and one chapter. Simon & Schuster mailed her a $250 advance, but no contract. They wanted to see more chapters. It took Carson another eighteen months to write five chapters (about 22,000 words) whereupon she received the contract and another $250.

After the contract for *Under the Sea-Wind* had been signed, Carson found that the writing moved more swiftly. Maria Carson, now seventy-one, delighted in typing the manuscript. Carson met her deadline date of December 31, 1940. After three years, Carson was both relieved and pleased to have the project completed.

In a letter to a friend enclosing some manuscript pages of the original longhand draft, Rachel Carson recalls her first experience in meeting a book publisher's deadline:

> In those concluding months of work on the book [fall of 1940] I often wrote late at night, in a large bedroom that occupied the entire second floor of our house on Flower Avenue. My constant companions during those otherwise solitary sessions were two precious Persian cats, Buzzie and Kito. Buzzie in particular used to sleep on my writing table, on the litter of notes and manuscript sheets. On two of these pages I had made sketches, first of his little head drooping with sleepiness, then of him after he had settled down comfortably for a nap.[26]

Additional Income Needed

During the writing and researching of *Under the Sea-Wind,* Carson still had to earn extra money, because $2,000, the income from her job at the Bureau of Fisheries, wasn't enough to support four people. And the publisher's small advances didn't allow her the luxury of writing *only* a book.

Rachel contributed many nature-related articles to the *Baltimore Sun* and to prominent periodicals such as *Nature, Reader's Digest,* the *New Yorker, Collier's, Coronet,* and *Transatlantic.* Her background in biology and zoology and her writing skill were helpful in earning supplemental income. Magazine articles continued to support Rachel for many years.

Would a published book change Carson's life? Carson could only hope that *Under the Sea-Wind* would please a large reading audience. She would find out ten months later.

Chapter

4 Work and Leisure Activities Mesh

On November 1, 1941, Carson's book *Under the Sea-Wind* was distributed to bookstores across the country. In addition, a cardboard box of copies was delivered to her home. The excited thirty-four-year-old author held the book in her hands, her heart beating wildly. She admired the glossy dust jacket bearing her name and sniffed the new ink, then cracked a book open to its dedication, "To My Mother,"[27] and handed it to the proud Maria. She also inscribed a book for her boss: "To Mr. Higgins, who started it all."[28]

In her first book, Carson told about life and survival among sea and shore animals by taking the reader through experiences of birds and fish. In one narrative she told the tragic story of snowy owls, Ookpik and his nesting mate, and their search for food and quest for survival from the ice-strewn sea edge across plains, forests, hills, and valleys of snow.

In another section of the book, the reader follows the life journey of Scomber the mackerel, from his beginnings as an egg in coastal waters, to helpless larva

In Under the Sea-Wind, *Carson tells a story of bitter survival of Ookpik, shown in this illustration by Bob Hines, preying upon a ptarmigan.*

carried by currents, to growing fish. Scomber's journey is marked by escape from swaying gill nets, large hungry tuna, stabbing birds, weighted seines [nets], and raiding dogfish until at long last the mackerel arrives in the deep, quiet waters along the edge of the continental shelf, where he will spend his adult years.

A migration of the Atlantic mackerel is described:

> Throughout all the latter part of April mackerel are rising from off the Virginia Capes and hurrying shoreward. . . . Some of the schools are small; some are as much as a mile wide and several miles long. . . . The mackerel are voiceless and they make no sound; yet their passage creates a heavy disturbance in the water. . . . As the mackerel hurry shoreward they swim in tier above tier. . . . In time the shoreward-running mackerel reach the inshore waters, where they ease their bodies of their burden of eggs and milt [sperm]. They leave in their wake a vast, sprawling river of life, the sea's counterpart of the river of stars that flows through the sky as the Milky Way.[29]

Throughout the chapters, Carson had readers experience ocean cycles of night and day, of seasons, of temperature changes. The forces of the ocean are interwoven with the life cycles of sea animals, birth through death.

Carson's writing style was particularly influenced by Henry Williamson, author of *Tarka the Otter*, and Henry Beston, who had written *The Outermost House*. Like Williamson, she used animals as central figures and told about their existence, both good times and hard times, in *Under the Sea-Wind*. She tried to imitate Beston's rhythm and flow with words as in his *The Outermost House*.

Carson had this comment about her favorite things to read:

> There was usually a volume of Thoreau's Journal or of Richard Jefferies' nature essays beside my bed, and I would relax my mind by reading a few pages before turning out the light. As might be expected, such great sea books as Tomlinson's *The Sea and the Jungle*, Beston's *Outermost House*, and [Melville's] *Moby Dick* are all favorite volumes.[30]

Reactions to *Under the Sea-Wind*

Unfortunately for Carson and her publishers, *Under the Sea-Wind* was released only a few weeks before December 7, 1941, the day of the Japanese attack on Pearl Harbor. Soon thereafter the nation was involved in World War II. People engrossed in the war effort were not interested in reading about migrating birds and fish. In the first year, *Under the Sea-Wind* sold 1,348 copies and then seemed to be forgotten. Six years later the sales total was still less than 1,600 copies. Carson earned less than a thousand dollars for three years of work.

Even though sales were disappointing, the scientific community was enthusiastic about the book. Well-known marine biologist and underseas explorer Dr. William Beebe, in a review for the magazine *Saturday Review of Literature*, said: "I have thoroughly enjoyed every word of the volume. . . . Miss Carson's science cannot be questioned."[31] True to his praise for

Ookpik, the Snowy Owl

In her book Under the Sea-Wind, *Carson describes survival techniques of snowbound owls living in the Arctic.*

"The snow death had taken many lives. It had visited the nest of two snowy owls in a ravine. . . . The hen had been brooding the six eggs for more than a week. During the first night of wild storm the snow had drifted deep about her, leaving a round depression like a stream-bed pothole in which she sat. All through the night the owl remained on the nest, warming the eggs. . . . By morning the snow was filling in around the feather-shod talons and creeping up around her sides. The cold was numbing, even through the feathers. At noon, with flakes like cotton shreds still flying in the sky, only the owl's head and shoulders were free of the snow. . . . Now, Ookpik, the cock owl, called to his mate with low, throaty cries. Numb and heavy-winged with cold, the hen roused and shook herself. It took many minutes to free herself from the snow and to climb, half fluttering, half stumbling, out of the nest, deep-walled with white. . . . The hen tried to fly but her heavy body flopped awkwardly in the snow for stiffness. When at last the slow circulation had crept back into her muscles, she rose into the air. . . .

As the snow fell on the still-warm eggs and the hard, bitter cold of the night gripped them, the life fires of the tiny embryos burned low. . . . The pulsating red sacs under the great oversized heads hesitated, beat spasmodically, and were stilled. The six little owls-to-be were dead in the snow."

her work, Dr. Beebe included two chapters from *Under the Sea-Wind* in his prestigious anthology, *The Book of Naturalists,* which Rachel considered an honor. This was the beginning of a long-lasting friendship.

Dr. Arthur A. Allen, an ornithologist, or bird specialist, at Cornell University, said, "The book will be as good ten years from now as it is today."[32] Carson was pleased, as well, with the review in the New York *Herald Tribune:* "There is drama in every sentence. She rouses our interest in this ocean world and we want to watch it."[33]

Although Carson was happy with the reviews, the book's disappointing sales caused her to advise an author friend:

> Instead of another book now, have you thought of doing some magazine

Marine biologist William Beebe is shown with a dusky shark. His praise for Under the Sea-Wind *gave Carson recognition in the scientific community.*

> articles? I am going to sound very materialistic, but after all if one is to live even in part by writing, he may as well look at the facts. Except for the rare miracles where a book becomes a "best seller," I am convinced that writing a book is a very poor gamble financially. This is based not only on my own experience (which, heaven knows, confirms it fully) but on what friends in the publishing business tell me. The average book will earn its author very little more than one magazine article placed with the "right" magazine.[34]

Carson told her friends she would never again put long hours into outside work that brought little reward.

After five years at her position with the Bureau of Fisheries, Carson was promoted from junior aquatic biologist to assistant aquatic biologist. To make room for wartime government agencies in Washington, her department was moved temporarily to Chicago. She and her mother reluctantly moved. Rachel's nieces Marjorie and Virginia, now out of high school, were old enough to be on their own.

During the war, the Bureau of Fisheries merged with the Bureau of Biological Survey and formed a branch of the U.S. Department of the Interior known as the Fish and Wildlife Service. Carson became responsible for a variety of official publications.

One of her assignments was to write pamphlets telling the public about the nutritional value of fish and shellfish. Giving expert advice on how to buy, prepare, and serve fish, Carson included recipes and cooking tips, which were used in magazines, newspapers, and on radio shows. Since meat was needed for the soldiers overseas, Carson's pamphlets were meant to encourage civilians to substitute fish in their diets. Using her biology background, Carson devoted large parts of the pamphlets to the life stories of specific fish: how and where they lived, their habits, their migration, and how they were caught.

Working in the Fish and Wildlife Service Bureau

In 1943 Carson returned to Washington, D.C., and was promoted to associate aquatic biologist. By 1945, she was promoted to aquatic biologist. Her assignments during the next ten years were to coordinate ideas, edit reports, and design publications. A year later, as information specialist, she did jobs in a broader category that included writing, editing, and making exhibits. In a total of sixteen years, owing to her competence, Carson had worked her way up the bureaucratic ladder to biologist and chief editor at the Fish and Wildlife Service.

Shirley Briggs, a graphic artist and writer, joined the service in 1945. She became a lifelong friend and sometime travel companion to Rachel. She recalled how Rachel kept the government job lively:

> Her qualities of zest and humor made even the dull stretches of bureaucratic procedure a matter for quiet fun, and she could instill a sense of adventure into the editorial routine of a government department.[35]

As World War II drew to a close, Rachel Carson, Shirley Briggs, and one other woman were the only females working for the Fish and Wildlife Service in nonclerical jobs.

Another colleague, too, had a high opinion of Carson's abilities. In 1948 when Bob Hines, a talented wildlife artist, joined the Fish and Wildlife Service, he hesitated to take the job since Carson, a woman, would be his supervisor. In later years Bob Hines had this to say about Carson:

> She was a very able executive with almost a man's administrative qualities. She knew how to get things done the quickest, simplest, most direct way.

Increasing Job Duties Consume Precious Writing Hours

In 1946 Carson was feeling restless with her government job. With responsibilities increasing at work, there was little time to write, and it would be risky to quit because she needed the money. In House of Life, *biographer Paul Brooks quotes Carson's complaints to a friend.*

"I don't know where I am going! I know that if I could choose what seems to me the ideal existence, it would be just to live by writing. But I have done far too little to dare risk it. And all the while my job with the Service grows and demands more and more of me, leaving less time that I could put on my own writing. And as my salary increases little by little, it becomes even more impossible to give it up! That is my problem right now, and not knowing what to do about it, I do nothing. For the past year or so I have told myself that the job (for the first time in my years with the Service) was giving me the travel I wanted and could not afford on my own and that, temporarily, was compensation for its other demands. But now the man higher up is leaving, and I may have to take his place, which will mean very close confinement to the office, I'm afraid."

She had the sweetest, quietest "no" any of us had ever heard. But it was like Gibraltar. You didn't move it. She had no patience with dishonesty or shirking in any form and she didn't appreciate anybody being dumb. But she always showed much more tolerance for a dull-minded person who was honest than for a bright one who wasn't. She didn't like shoddy work or shoddy behavior. She was just so doggone good she couldn't see why other people couldn't try to be the same. She had *standards*, high ones.[36]

Conservation in Action

When the war ended, the Fish and Wildlife Service tried to revive public efforts in conservation. As editor-in-chief of the publishing operations of the government agency, Carson was given the responsibility for a new series of twelve booklets entitled "Conservation in Action." The booklets represented an attempt to educate the public on the significance of conserving natural resources and maintaining the ecological integrity of places where plants and animals live, including the three hundred U.S. national wildlife refuges.

Carson's philosophy for the project stressed the ecological point of view, which was not a common stance during the late 1940s:

> The Western Hemisphere has a relatively short history of the exploitation of its natural resources by man. This history, though short, contains many chapters of reckless waste and appalling destruction. Entire species of animals

Carson searches the sky for birds as she sits atop Pennsylvania's Hawk Mountain in 1945.

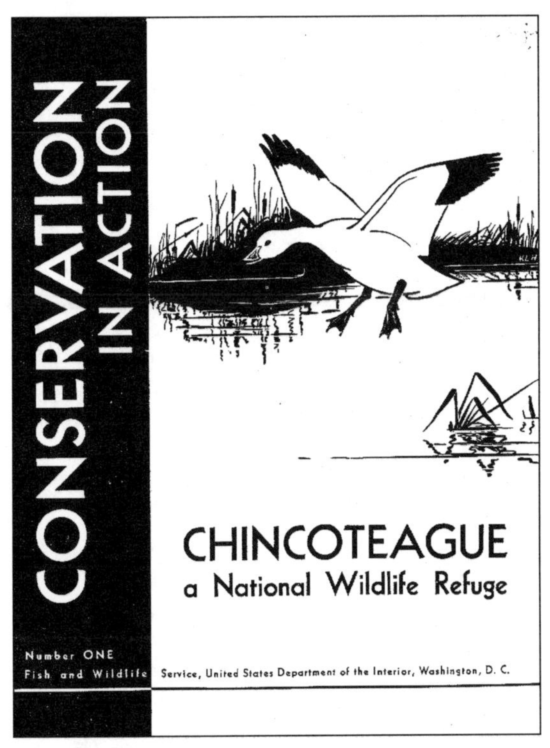

Written and designed by Carson, this booklet was the first in a series published by the Fish and Wildlife Service in 1947.

> have been exterminated, or reduced to so small a remnant that their survival is doubtful. Forests have been despoiled by uncontrolled and excessive cutting of lumber, grasslands have been destroyed by overgrazing. . . . Wildlife, water, forests, grasslands all are parts of man's essential environment. . . . We in the United States have been slow to learn that our wildlife, like other forms of natural wealth, must be vigorously protected if we are to continue to enjoy its benefits.[37]

As editor-in-chief, Carson had a spacious office with two walls lined with bookcases. She supervised authors and six members of the Fish and Wildlife Service staff, who did the illustrating, layouts, design, and editing of publications, including the "Conservation in Action" booklets.

Carson Relished Her On-the-Job Research Trips

Carson wrote half the booklets and edited the others. To make the booklets accurate, field research was required. In visiting eastern fisheries, aquatic wildlife refuges, and the California coast of the Pacific, Carson finally could get out of the office. Colleague Shirley Briggs accompanied her on some trips. They traveled to Chincoteague Wildlife Refuge in Virginia for one booklet. Other trips included Plum Island off the coast of Massachusetts and Mattamuskeet Refuge in North Carolina. Other pleasurable research hours were spent on bird-watching expeditions along the Potomac River, in city parks, and on Hawk Mountain in Pennsylvania. Shirley Briggs recalled:

> A foray along the shore or through the spruce woods [with Carson] was always high adventure. We who were included in [Rachel's] expeditions learned a great deal about many aspects of our world, but most of all a way of seeing, alert for every impression, with keen delight in all manner of small creatures as well as the vast horizons and far reaches.[38]

In a 1949 assignment, Carson had to write about the bureau's research ship *Albatross III*, which was anchored at Woods Hole. The government was concerned about a drop in the population of several species of commercial fish. Carson felt that the experience of being on the fishing trawler/science lab would make for a more interesting and accurate article. Thus she and Marie Rodell, her friend and literary agent, became the first women allowed on such a trip. They were not welcomed by the crew, however, for many sailors believed that women on a ship brought bad luck. The ten-day rugged adventure took place in the North Atlantic waters of Georges Bank, a famous fishing ground that lies two hundred miles east of Boston, Massachusetts, and south of Nova Scotia. Carson observed the crew taking depth surveys and watched as the ocean terrain was charted. She heard sonar echoes bouncing off fish schools. Carson watched with excitement as groaning machines dragged in heavy nets filled with fish, crabs, sponges, starfish, and other sea life from the ocean floor. Then she dissected the various sea animals and examined them under a microscope. Despite heavy fog, seasickness, bad food, and noisy machinery, the sights, sounds, and smells of the open sea gave Carson enthusiasm about a new book.

Carson always had her binoculars with her on nature walks for magnified views of the natural wonders around her.

The Plunge to Do a Second Book

Carson was frustrated with her growing job responsibilities, which left her little time to write. Looking for a different challenge and more time for herself, she asked the National Audubon Society to keep her in mind if a position opened up. She also applied, unsuccessfully, for an editorial job with the *Reader's Digest.* Yet Carson couldn't shake the urge to write another book. She wanted to write a biography of the ocean, from the surface to its depths and its mysterious floor.

In 1948, when she started the ambitious project, she wrote a friend:

> I am impressed by man's dependence upon the ocean, directly, and in thousands of ways unsuspected by most people. These relationships, and my belief that we will become even more dependent upon the ocean as we destroy the land, are really the themes of this book.[39]

Her goal was to include the oceanographic research accomplished during the war. She wanted to relate this scientific information in easily understood language.

After Carson had written about one-third of the book and an outline, her agent, Marie Rodell, obtained a contract with Oxford University Press.

Aware of Carson's financial problems, her friend explorer William Beebe recommended her for a Eugene F. Saxton Memorial Fellowship, which provided assistance to creative writers. With the $2,250 grant, Carson took an unpaid leave of absence from her government job to complete the new book.

An Anxious Sea Dive

To give validation to her research, Carson was advised by Beebe to experience a deep sea dive. Not being a good swimmer, however, Carson approached this venture with some anxiety and asked her colleague Shirley Briggs to accompany her. Normal diving gear in those days included lead weights on the feet, a bulky rubber suit, and a huge metal helmet. Carson made several shallow dives in the Florida Keys. Although she went down only fifteen feet to the coral reefs, she was amazed at what she saw:

> I learned what the surface of the water looks like underneath and how exquisitely delicate and varied are the colors displayed by the animals of the reef, and I got the feeling of the misty green vistas of a strange, nonhuman world.[40]

"You don't go very deep unless you are an experienced diver," Carson explained later. "I was a little nervous, too, because the mechanics are a bit involved for a novice. And the sound of air coming into the helmet is not very pleasant."[41]

Besides her undersea experience for her contracted second book, Carson had consulted at least a thousand separate printed sources, corresponded with oceanographers, talked to specialists, and sought help from many librarians. Through her government job, Carson had contact with ocean specialists both in America and abroad and she didn't hesitate to ask them to verify her data. To one

Carson, on the University of Miami research boat Nauplius, *sails to the Florida Keys for her coral reef dives.*

expert, Arthur McBride, curator of the Marine Studios in Florida, she wrote:

> To say that I am grateful for your help is a vast understatement, but somehow the English language seems inadequate to thank a man who spent his fourth of July writing by hand—a 16-page letter in answer to the questions of a stranger. If I had had any idea you would give me such a wealth of detail I would have lacked the courage to ask so many questions, but the material was exactly what I needed.[42]

Landlubbers Experience the High Seas

For research, Carson, accompanied by her agent Marie Rodell, ventured on a rugged ship, the Albatross III. *This excerpt from Marie's diary, quoted in* House of Life, *by Paul Brooks, documents the women's introduction to the vessel.*

"Woods Hole, 7/26/49—I arrived in Woods Hole at four-thirty; Rachel met me at the station and took me to the Residence, where we were to spend the night—a grim old wooden structure that houses the employees of the U.S. Fisheries labs. After supper, we went round to the wharf and had our first look at the *Albatross III.*

No one could call her pretty. The forward well was heaped with the nets; at the invitation of the third mate, who introduced himself, we clambered over them and were taken up to the wheelhouse. All the modern improvements: Loran radio direction finder, ship-to-shore radio telephone, Sperry gyroscope compass; depth recorder. The third mate filled up our ears with horror stories, 'Always hang on to something,' he warned us; 'the water coming over the decks can bang you about a lot.' From the wheelhouse, he pointed down to an open hatch in the center of the forward deck; we could see a spindly ladder leading down. 'That's where you eat,' he said, and bowed us off the ship with sadistic pleasure. We then went over to see Rachel's friends the Goltsoffs; he is the world's foremost expert on oysters. He spent a happy hour regaling us with the horrors that have befallen the *Albatross* and those aboard her—broken noses, smashed hands—'Never a trip without an accident,' he said happily. I was by now in a full-fledged panic, even though I knew everyone was doing this deliberately. We fell asleep that night planning what food to take aboard so we wouldn't have to go down that ladder in a storm. What a pair of landlubbers!"

Colleague Bob Hines often accompanied Rachel on research trips. Here they collect tide specimens along the Florida Keys.

Carson comments about her research:

People often ask me how long I worked on *The Sea Around Us.* I usually reply that in a sense I have been working on it all my life, although the actual writing of the book occupied only about three years. As a very small child I was fascinated by the ocean, although I had never seen it. I dreamed of it and longed to see it, and I read all the sea literature I could find. . . . The eagerness of [many] people to help [me] was really a very heartwarming experience.[43]

Previews of *The Sea Around Us*

To generate interest in *The Sea Around Us,* literary agent Marie Rodell offered chapters to various magazines. *Yale Review* published one chapter, "Birth of an Island," which later was awarded a $1,000 prize as best science writing in 1950. *Nature* magazine and *Reader's Digest,* which paid Carson $10,000, also published parts of the book. However, at least a dozen other magazines, including *Harper's, National Geographic,*

Carson's second book, The Sea Around Us, *tells about the diversified elements of the sea. This is a view of an underwater coral reef.*

and the *Saturday Evening Post,* turned down chapters. Finally an editor at the *New Yorker* became enthusiastic about the chapters and roughly half the book was published in that magazine in the spring of 1951. Carson's payment from the *New Yorker* equaled almost a year's salary at her government job. The appearance in this prestigious magazine of a series of three articles, called "Profiles of the Sea," had an enormous effect on Carson's writing career. Moreover, the *New Yorker* was flooded with complimentary letters about the essays.

When *The Sea Around Us* was published in July 1951, it quickly climbed the *New York Times* best-seller list—and stayed there for eighty-six straight weeks. This was a new record for best-sellers. Rachel became instantly famous.

Chapter

5 Wondrous Senses

The public demand for Carson's book, *The Sea Around Us*, forced Oxford University Press to make duplicate printing plates so two printing presses could operate at the same time. Readers were impressed by Carson's ability to bring the mysterious sea into the realm of popular understanding. Carson's intense research showed her vast knowledge and understanding, as well as her ability to translate scientific facts into enjoyable reading material.

In her second book, *The Sea Around Us,* Carson described the many parts of the sea: the surface, the sunless floor, the islands and how they are born, and the moving tides, which are controlled by the moon, the sun, the winds, and the ocean currents.

The Sea Around Us Book Excerpts

For example, in the chapter entitled "The Birth of an Island," Carson explained how islands come about:

> Millions of years ago, a volcano built a mountain on the floor of the Atlantic. In eruption after eruption the lava mountain grew, reaching up toward the surface of the sea. It came to measure a hundred miles across its base. Finally the cone of the volcano emerged as an island with an area of about two hundred square miles. Thousands of years passed, and thousands of thousands. Eventually the waves of the Atlantic cut down the cone and reduced it to a shoal—all of it, that is, but a small fragment which remained above water. This fragment we know as Bermuda.[44]

In another section Carson defined the wholeness of all the oceans:

> So, clearly, there is no such thing as water that is wholly of the Pacific or wholly of the Atlantic, or of the Indian or of the Antarctic Ocean. The surf that we enjoy at Virginia Beach or at Miami or at Monterey today may have lapped at the base of Antarctic icebergs or sparkled in the Mediterranean sun, years ago, before it moved through dark and unseen waterways to the place we find it now. It is by the deep, hidden currents that the oceans are made one.[45]

In the July 7, 1951, issue of *Saturday Review of Literature*, commentator Austin H. Clark wrote:

> Rare indeed is the individual who can present a comprehensive and well-balanced picture of such a complex entity as the sea in an easy and fluent style and in terms anyone can understand. Rachel Carson is such an individual.[46]

Having *The Sea Around Us* on the *New York Times* best-seller list made the forty-four-year-old author a celebrity and led to speaking engagements, awards, and traveling, plus lots of fan mail to answer. People wrote to Carson saying they liked her book because it took them away from the stress and strain of human problems. The writer recalled:

> In publishing the book, Oxford University Press didn't foresee all this clamor and failed to put my picture on the jacket. So the field was open for all sorts of speculation—what did I look like, how old was I, how did I happen to discover the sea?
>
> Among male readers there was a certain reluctance to acknowledge that a woman could have dealt with a scientific subject. Some, who apparently had never read the Bible enough to know that Rachel is a woman's name, wrote: "I assume from the author's knowledge that he must be a man." Another, addressing me properly as *Miss* Rachel Carson, nevertheless began his letter "Dear Sir:". He explained his salutation by saying that he had always been convinced that the males possess

The National Book Award winners for the most distinguished work of 1951 included Marianne Moore for her Collected Poems, *James Jones for his novel* From Here to Eternity, *and Rachel Carson for her best-seller* The Sea Around Us. *The toastmaster at the ceremony was author-lecturer John Mason Brown.*

Rachel's Lifelong Passion for Cats

Rachel Carson sometimes talked or wrote about cats as if they were human beings. In House of Life, *biographer Paul Brooks quotes from a letter Rachel wrote to the Cat Welfare Association while she was working on* The Edge of the Sea.

"I have always found that a cat has a truly great capacity for friendship. He asks only that we respect his personal rights and his individuality; in return, he gives his devotion, understanding, and companionship. Cats are extremely sensitive to the joys and sorrows of their human friends, they share our interests.

For almost 20 years we had in our home a wonderful family of Persians—the mother and her three children. They lived to the ages of 11, 8, 13, and 16 respectively. Buzzie and Kito helped me write *Under the Sea-Wind,* taking turns lying on the manuscript beside my typewriter far into the nights. Tippy did the same for *The Sea Around Us* more recently. Now they are all gone. A little all-gray kitten named Muffin came into our home last September at the age of six weeks. He has now become a full-fledged associate with me on the book I'm now writing—a guide to the seashore. Since the middle of March he has traveled about 2000 miles with my mother and me."

the supreme intellectual powers of the world, and he could not bring himself to reverse his conviction.[47]

For Carson, who was a shy, private person, fame was not always a pleasant experience. She wrote about one incident that happened when she was promoting *The Sea Around Us:*

It never occurred to me, for example, that people would go to great lengths just to have a look at someone whose book was a best seller. A few months after *The Sea* was published, I was on a long southern field trip for my new book. In a strange town, I went into a beauty shop, and while I was sitting under the drier—which until then I had considered an inviolate sanctuary—the proprietor came over, turned off the drier, and said: "I hope you don't mind, but there is someone who wants to meet you." I admit I felt hardly at my best, with a towel around my neck and my hair in pin curls.[48]

The Sea Around Us received many awards and honors. One was the National Book Award for the best nonfiction in 1951. Another was the John Burroughs Medal for a nature book of high literary merit. There were awards from the New

Carson examines a tide pool near her home in Maine.

York Zoological Society, the *New York Times*, and the *Reader's Digest*, as well.

Carson, herself, was esteemed for her work. She received four honorary degrees: one from her alma mater, the Pennsylvania College for Women; the second from Oberlin College in Oberlin, Ohio; the third from Smith College in Northampton, Massachusetts; and the fourth from Drexel Institute of Technology in Philadelphia. She was elected to the National Institute of Arts and Letters, which is a significant honor in the United States. She was voted "Woman of the Year in Literature" by the nation's newspapers and also accepted the Henry G. Bryant Medal of the Philadelphia Geographical Society (the first ever granted to a woman) for distinguished geographical service.

The book also led to friendships with marine scientists all over the world, whose approval of her work was deeply satisfying to Carson. One letter she received from Gustaf Arrhenius, a leading marine scientist in Sweden, read in part:

> Before having seen your book I was somewhat skeptical because I have never before seen any successful popular treatment of this subject, or rather, this immense amount of subjects. But unluckily enough, I started to read it; unluckily because I have some very urgent work just at this moment and once I started with your book I couldn't possibly finish [my work], that fascinating did I find it from the first page to the last. . . . I felt obliged to write to you to express my admiration. . . . Again, congratulations to your masterpiece.[49]

In less than a year, the 230-page book sold more than 200,000 copies. After endless autograph parties, receptions, award ceremonies, and speaking engagements, Carson wrote to her agent, Marie Rodell:

> All of these invitations, no matter how pleasant, would absolutely wreck the writing program I am now laying out. What has gone on in the last six

months is all very fine, but enough is enough! . . . In Cleveland and in Pittsburgh I was left at the mercy of a bunch of eager beavers who thought only of how many minutes the day contained and how many events they could cram into it, and as a result I came home in a state of utter exhaustion. I will not submit to anything like that again.[50]

Eventually *The Sea Around Us* sold a million book copies in the United States and was translated into thirty-two languages.

Success Leads to More Success

Because of the success of *The Sea Around Us,* Oxford University Press acquired publishing rights to *Under the Sea-Wind* from Simon & Schuster and put out a new unillustrated edition of Carson's neglected first book. *Sea-Wind* was very well received and quickly became a best-seller, too.

Carson sold the movie rights for *The Sea Around Us* to RKO studios. The project became a nightmare, however, when Carson read the rewritten Hollywood script and saw the film. She and Marie Rodell submitted a long list of scientific errors to be corrected. In spite of the inaccuracies that remained in the finished work, the movie won an Oscar for the best full-length documentary of 1953.

By June 1952, with her checks from magazine excerpts and book royalties, Carson felt financially secure. In that month, she officially resigned her position at the Fish and Wildlife Service and began to devote her time to doing what made her happy: travel, research, and writing. She already had ideas for her third contracted book, which would describe sea animals: where they lived and why, their adaptations to their environment, how they got food, their life cycle, and their predators, competitors, and allies.

Carson could now afford a dreamed-of shoreline summer home, and she purchased 1.5 acres at West Southport on the

Carson's summer cottage in Maine as viewed from the rocky Boothbay Harbor shore.

Helping Children to "Sense" Nature

A few suggestions excerpted from Rachel Carson's book, The Sense of Wonder, *show her enthusiasm for sharing simple wonders of nature with children.*

"If a child is to keep alive his inborn sense of wonder without any such gift from the fairies, he needs the companionship of at least one adult who can share it, rediscovering with him the joy, excitement, and mystery of the world we live in. . . . If you are a parent who feels he has little nature lore at his disposal, there is still much you can do for your child. With him, wherever you are and whatever your resources, you can still look up at the sky—its dawn and twilight beauties, its moving clouds, its stars by night. You can listen to the wind, whether it blows with majestic voice through a forest or sings a many-voiced chorus around the eaves of your house or the corners of your apartment building, and in the listening, you can gain magical release for your thoughts. You can still feel the rain on your face and think of its long journey . . . from sea to air to earth. Even if you are a city dweller, you can find some place, perhaps a park or a golf course, where you can observe the mysterious migrations of the birds and the changing seasons. And with your child you can ponder the mystery of a growing seed, even if it be only one planted in a pot of earth in the kitchen window."

Rachel takes pleasure in sharing nature walks with her grand-nephew, Roger Christie.

Maine seacoast. There, in a cottage she had built on a rocky cliff along the west shore of Booth Bay Harbor, she fulfilled her yearning to be near the sea and its sounds. From the many windows of her cottage, Rachel could see wildflowers and evergreen trees in the front and the sea in the back. A steep wooden staircase led down the cliff to a small beach and tide pools, with a wondrous variety of sea life to enjoy and study. The cottage had paneled walls, and Rachel used one room as her study with a built-in desk, bookcases, and a worktable for her microscope. With the sea at her back door, this was a perfect place for writing.

Half a mile down the shore of Rachel's summer cottage lived Stanley and Dorothy Freeman, who were admirers of Rachel's books and became her close friends. The Freemans had a winter home in West Bridgewater, Massachusetts, and had similar nature interests.

Eternal Wonders of Nature

The Freemans joined Rachel, her mother, and Bob Hines on beach picnics. Dorothy and Stanley took the group sailing on their sixteen-foot sloop. From sunrises to sunsets, high tides and low tides, Rachel bathed herself in the beauty and wonder of her ocean paradise and lab. Each day brought the excitement of studying sea anemones, pink coralline algae, barnacle shells, tiny worms, seaweed, and minute crustaceans. She fell asleep to the lullaby of the surf in a moon-brightened room.

Near her cottage, Rachel sits between her neighbor friends, Dorothy and Stanley Freeman, who shared her intense interest in nature.

During the summer of 1954, Rachel worked on an illustrated lecture with Stanley Freeman. Stanley took all the photographs that were used in the colored slide presentation. The fall lecture was for the Audubon Society in Washington, and the demand for tickets was so great that the lecture had to be presented twice.

At summer's end, Rachel always found it sad to leave the cottage and return to Silver Spring and the dreary winter months. Early one October, she wrote:

> The autumn color is becoming vivid everywhere; the blueberry bushes above my shore are all afire. . . . All the color suddenly became far more intense than it had been so that it is really breathtaking. I'm so glad we stayed to see it. And almost every morning our trees are full of small bird migrants that have come in during the night, so that breakfast has to be eaten with the binoculars in one hand.[51]

Research Traveling

Research on the third book actually began before *The Sea Around Us* came out. In October 1950, Carson had applied for a $4,000 Guggenheim Fellowship. The fellowship, which would enable her to take another leave of absence from her job, was received in April 1951. After the success of her book later that year, however, she returned the money. In the summer of 1951, she began traveling to do her research.

With her mother and one cat, Muffy, Carson drove about 2,000 miles exploring for this proposed book, *The Edge of the Sea.* They went to Florida coral beaches, North Carolina beaches, Cape Cod, and the Maine coast.

At Carson's suggestion, the Boston publisher Houghton Mifflin offered Fish and Wildlife artist Bob Hines a contract to illustrate her book. Bob had from time

Carson never tired of exploring tide pools.

Bob Hines scrapes specimens from a sea wall in the Florida Keys for Carson to examine under a microscope.

to time accompanied Carson and her mother to the Maine beaches. Sometimes Carson stood so long in the icy Atlantic tide pools that her legs grew numb and Bob had to carry her out.

He described some excursions:

> We'd go out on the mud flats. She'd scrounge around to find what she wanted. We'd bring the stuff back in a bucket and I'd make the drawings. Then Rachel would put them back in the bucket and return them to their natural places on the beach.[52]

Recalling the years Carson and he worked together on the book, Bob said:

> She had a subdued sense of humor. The impression of her laughter is more vivid than any detail of its causes. They were small unmemorable things. All I can remember is her beautiful tinkling laugh in moments when she felt strongly the enjoyment of being alive. It was good to hear her laugh.[53]

After four years of research, travel, and writing and painful rewriting, Carson's new book was ready to be released.

Another Best-Seller

The Edge of the Sea, published in the fall of 1955, focused on the ecology of sea creatures and how they live in a community. In the preface Carson wrote:

> True understanding demands intuitive comprehension of the whole life of the creature that once inhabited [an] empty shell [for example]: how it survived amid surf and storms, what were its enemies, how it found food and reproduced its kind, what were its relations to the particular sea world in which it lived.[54]

Carson described the sea's edge as beautiful and fascinating. The rocky coast, sandy beaches, and coral reefs were the settings for her chapters:

Carson poses for a portrait taken about the time her third book, The Edge of the Sea, *was published.*

> Small, dingy snails move about over rocks that are slippery with the growth of infinitesimal green plants; the snails scraping, scraping, scraping to find food before the surf returns.[55]

In a later chapter, she observed:

> It is an extraordinary thing to watch the sand come to life if one happens to be wading where there is a large colony of [mole] crabs. One moment it may seem uninhabited. Then, in that fleeting instant when the water of a receding wave flows seaward like a thin stream of liquid glass, there are suddenly hundreds of little gnome-like faces peering through the sandy floor—beady-eyed, long whiskered faces set in bodies so nearly the color of their background that they can barely be seen. And when, almost instantly, the faces fade back into invisibility . . . [one senses] that there was merely an apparition induced by the magical quality of this world of shifting sand and foaming water.[56]

The Edge of the Sea was on the best-seller list for twenty-three weeks. Portions of it also appeared in a two-part "Profile" in the *New Yorker,* and a condensed form was published in *Reader's Digest.* The material received favorable reviews. This book, different from her first two, was written in the companionship of three close friends: Bob Hines, who did 160 illustrations, and the Freemans, to whom the book was dedicated:

> To Dorothy and Stanley Freeman, who have gone down with me into the low-tide world and have felt its beauty and mystery.[57]

The Edge of the Sea brought Carson two more honors: the $2,500 Achievement Award of the American Association of University Women for outstanding woman scholar and a citation of "outstanding book of the year" from the National Council of Women of the United States. Fame did not change her life. Carson still enjoyed the familiar things—her friends, her family, and her summer cottage.

Sharing Nature

Rachel had developed a special relationship with her toddler grandnephew, Roger Christie. He was Marjorie's son, and whenever mother and child visited the beach cottage, Rachel took Roger to explore their surroundings. They spent many hours on the beach feeling the cool breezy wind and salt spray, watching beach critters, and in the evenings, flashlights in hands, searching for ghost crabs.

Rachel wrote about their adventures in a magazine article "Help Your Child to Wonder," which first appeared in *Woman's Home Companion* magazine in 1956. The purpose of the article was to show adults simple ways to expose children to the awe-someness of nature. Carson stated:

> The lasting pleasures of contact with the natural world are not reserved for

A Firefly Flashes at Sparkling Phosphorescence

In a letter to Dorothy and Stanley Freeman, who were not in Maine at the time, Rachel shared an evening of excitement at her cottage. This excerpt from the letter is taken from House of Life, *Paul Brooks's biography of Carson.*

"I have to tell you about something strange and wonderful. . . . We are now having the spring tides of the new moon, you know, and they have traced their advance well over my beach the past several nights. There had been lots of swell and surf noise all day, so it was most exciting down there toward midnight. . . . Of course you can guess the surf was full of diamonds and emeralds, and was throwing them on the wet sand by the dozen . . . phosphorescence. The individual sparks were so large—we'd see them glowing in the sand, or sometimes caught in the in-and-out play of water, just riding back and forth. . . . Now here is where my story becomes different. Once, glancing up, I said . . . jokingly, 'Look—one of them has taken to the air!' A firefly was going by, his lamp blinking. We thought nothing special of it, but in a few minutes one of us said, 'There's that firefly again.' The next time he really got a reaction from us, for he was flying so low over the water that his light cast a long surface reflection, like a little headlight. Then the truth dawned on me. He 'thought' the flashes in the water were other fireflies, signaling to him in the age-old manner of fireflies! Sure enough, he was soon in trouble and we saw his light flashing urgently as he was rolled around in the wet sand. . . . You can guess the rest: I waded in and rescued him and put him in Roger's bucket to dry his wings. . . . I have never seen any account, scientifically, of fireflies responding to other phosphorescence. I suppose I should write it up briefly for some journal if it actually isn't known."

Rachel adopted her grandnephew, Roger, after his mother died in 1957.

> scientists but are available to anyone who will place himself under the influence of earth, sea and sky and their amazing life.[58]

After Rachel's death, the article was published in book form in *The Sense of Wonder.*

Illness Leads to New Responsibilities

The summer of 1956, when Rachel was nearly fifty herself, was spent driving her mother and her niece to local clinics. Marie, now eighty-seven and crippled with arthritis, contracted pneumonia and was ill for four months. Marjorie also was disabled with arthritis, as well as diabetes. Early in 1957, Marjorie came down with pneumonia and had to be hospitalized. Two weeks later, Marjorie died in the hospital.

In April Rachel shared her sadness with friend and editor, Paul Brooks, in a letter:

> Marjorie and I were very close all her life, and of course I miss her dreadfully. Among the many changes this has brought is the fact that I shall now adopt Roger as my own; he had lost his father before he could remember him, and in our small family I am the logical one to care for him and, I'm sure, the one who is really closest to him. He does not fully realize the finality of his loss, and seems quite happy with us. But it is not an easy undertaking—I should be 15 to 20 years younger![59]

After Marjorie's death, Carson had a home built in the suburbs of Silver Spring, Maryland, on a secluded one-acre lot. The new house fit her new family circle requirements. During that summer of 1957, Carson helped with the editing and layout of a juvenile edition of *The Sea Around Us.*

The year 1958 was the beginning of a huge four-year project for Carson, which brought her controversy. It also planted the seeds of today's environmental movement.

Chapter

6 Songbirds Are Silenced

Carson's new project was fueled by a letter from a friend, Olga Owens Huckins, who lived in Duxbury, Massachusetts, a small town between Boston and Cape Cod. Olga and her husband had created a bird sanctuary on their property, but in the summer of 1957 the area had been sprayed heavily with DDT (dichlorodiphenyl trichloroethane) to control mosquitoes. Writing in January 1958, Olga Huckins described finding dead birds all over the property after the spraying. She asked Rachel for help in stopping the spraying because she hoped that Rachel would know the right people in Washington to consult for help.

That letter was a leading factor in Carson's decision to put aside an invitation to do a book about the continents for Harper & Brothers. The letter was far too disturbing to ignore. Carson had been concerned with the use of DDT as long

A low-flying plane releases chemicals to rid crops of pests.

ago as 1945, when it was being used to control pests on farms. At that time she had queried *Reader's Digest,* offering to write an article about the dangers of DDT spraying. Experiments in the use of DDT were being conducted in Maryland, and Carson had wanted to write about effects of the poison. She also intended to find out whether the extensive use of the pesticide upset the delicate balance of nature. The *Reader's Digest* was not interested in the proposed article.

DDT Warnings

In the mid-1940s biologists and ecologists had issued warnings about DDT. For example, in December 1944, the American Association of Economic Entomologists reported:

> DDT will not kill all important insect pests. It will kill many beneficial insects which are allies of mankind against the destructive species. Because of its toxicity to a wide variety of insects, its large-scale use might create problems which do not now exist.[60]

In 1945, in an article in *Harper's,* a member of the Department of Agriculture stated that entomologists

> do not view DDT as an unmixed blessing and they will not go off the deep end in recommending its use in agriculture until they know a lot more about it.[61]

Also in 1945, the *New Yorker* quoted author and former president of the New York Entomological Society, Edwin Way Teale:

> A spray as indiscriminate [random] as DDT can upset the economy of nature as much as a revolution upsets social economy. Ninety per cent of all insects are good, and if they are killed, things go out of kilter right away.[62]

Zoo workers spray a pest-beleaguered elephant with DDT in 1945. At the time, the consequences of such spraying were not fully known.

The Letter That Started It All

Here is part of the letter that is credited with prompting Carson to write Silent Spring. *The sadness of birds dying awful deaths from uncontrolled DDT spraying and the plea for help from her friend, Olga Owens Huckins, moved Carson to action. Mrs. Huckins's words, quoted by John Henricksson in* Rachel Carson: The Environmental Movement, *accomplished their purpose.*

"The mosquito control plane flew over our small town last summer. Since we live close to the marshes, we were treated to several lethal doses as the pilot crisscrossed our place. And we consider the spraying of active poison over private land to be a serious aerial intrusion.

The 'harmless' shower bath killed seven of our lovely songbirds outright. We picked up three dead bodies the next morning right by the door. They were birds that had lived close to us, trusted us, and built their nests in our trees year after year. The next day, three were scattered around the bird bath. (I had emptied it and scrubbed it after the spraying but YOU CAN NEVER KILL DDT.) On the following day one robin dropped suddenly from a branch in our woods. We were too heartsick to hunt for other corpses. All of these birds died horribly, and in the same way. Their bills were gaping open, and their splayed claws were drawn up to their breasts in agony.

Air spraying where it is not needed or wanted is inhuman, undemocratic, and probably unconstitutional. For those of us who stand helplessly on the tortured earth, it is intolerable."

During the next thirteen years, Carson continued to follow pesticide spraying in the press and in governmental reports. In the summer of 1957 a court case publicized a shocking misuse of pesticides. DDT was sprayed in Long Island to eradicate the gypsy moth and the case came to trial in New York. Parts of Nassau and Suffolk counties in Long Island were drenched with DDT from the air. Carson later wrote that this was a ridiculous use of pesticides, because New York city could not possibly have a serious moth infestation problem. The gypsy moth is a forest insect, certainly not an inhabitant of cities. Nor does it live in meadows, cultivated fields, gardens, or marshes. Nevertheless, the planes hired by the United States Department of Agriculture and the New York Department of Agriculture and Markets in 1957 showered down the prescribed DDT-in-fuel-oil with impartiality. They sprayed truck gardens and dairy farms, fish ponds and salt marshes. They sprayed the quarter-acre lots of suburbia, drench-

Riding a tractor, a farmer sprays pesticide on his cornfield.

ing a housewife making a desperate effort to cover her garden before the roaring plane reached her, and showering insecticide over children at play and commuters at railway stations. At Setauket [on Long Island] a fine quarter horse drank from a trough in a field which the planes had sprayed; ten hours later it was dead. Automobiles were spotted with the oily mixture; flowers and shrubs were ruined. Birds, fish, crabs, and useful insects were killed.[63]

With failed court injunctions to halt the spraying, the case was carried all the way to the Supreme Court, which declined to hear it.

Scientific evidence proving DDT's dangers continued to build up. In 1958 the U.S. government stepped in because huge fish kills were discovered: more than 60,000 dead in a lake after an orange grove spraying and more than 71,000 dead in a creek after a cotton field spraying. Congress ordered the Department of the Interior to study the effects of pesticides on fish and wildlife.

Through her research, Carson discovered that besides DDT, other poisons such as dieldrin (twenty times as toxic as DDT) and parathion were being used:

> So dangerous is [parathion] that physicians and first aid workers handling victims of the poisonous spraying are cautioned to wear rubber gloves while removing patient's clothing.[64]

As Rachel did more research on the poisonous chemicals, she decided to use magazine articles to call attention to the dangers of random spraying to wildlife and public health.

Four publications turned her proposal down: *Reader's Digest, Ladies' Home Journal, Woman's Home Companion,* and *Good Housekeeping.* An editor from *Good Housekeeping* had asked the magazine's chemical analysis laboratory to respond:

> It is our feeling that the article proposed by Miss Rodell [Carson's agent] is something which we should under no circumstances consider. We doubt whether many of the things outlined in this letter could be substantiated. . . . No single case of human poisoning from DDT has been documented. . . . Such an article would bring "unwarranted fear."[65]

Since no one would publish a magazine article, Carson considered contributing a chapter to a book to be written by someone else. Because Carson was busy raising Roger, she didn't want to take on a whole book project herself. However,

Reader's Digest Rejects Information on Pesticides

On July 15, 1945, Carson had tried to interest Reader's Digest *in an article about the dangers of widespread use of pesticides. This excerpt from her proposal is found in Paul Brooks's biography,* House of Life.

"Here is a query for your consideration—Practically at my back door here in Maryland, an experiment of more than ordinary interest and importance is going on. We have all heard a lot about what DDT will soon do for us by wiping out insect pests. The experiments at Patuxent have been planned to show what other effects DDT may have if applied to wide areas: what it will do to insects that are beneficial or even essential; how it may affect waterfowl, or birds that depend on insect food; whether it may upset the whole delicate balance of nature if unwisely used.

I believe there is a timely story in these tests. The incredible amount of painstaking work involved in setting up the test areas, the methods, results, and the interpretation from the biologist's point of view should add up to a pretty good article. It's something that really does affect everybody.

I am in a position to cover the progress of the thing at first hand during the coming weeks, and with a little encouragement from you, I should do so with a view to turning out an article aimed for the pages of the *Digest.* The background is pretty well sketched in the enclosed release. Does the idea interest you?"

Carson spends time on her beach in Maine contemplating how she will write about the misuse of pesticides.

other writers approached to do the book insisted that Carson was the person to write it. A well-known author, she had established scientific credibility and had important government contacts.

Ready to confront the truth, Carson wrote:

> I may not like what I see, but it does no good to ignore it. . . . So it seems time someone wrote of life in the light of the truth as it now appears to us. And I think that may be the book I am to write.[66]

Rachel recalled later:

> The more I learned about the use of pesticides the more appalled I became. I realized that here was the material for a book. What I discovered was that everything which meant most to me as a naturalist was being threatened, and that nothing I could do would be more important. However, I wanted to do more than merely express concern: I wanted to demonstrate that that concern was well founded.[67]

In May 1958 Carson signed a contract with Houghton Mifflin for a short book about the misuse of pesticides. However, her research material continued to multiply.

Carson Hires an Assistant

Carson used all 2,000 pages of transcripts of expert testimony from the so-called gypsy moth trial in New York to establish many contacts in the medical and agricultural fields. She wrote and telephoned scientists and experts who knew about pesticides. To help handle the enormous amount of correspondence, Carson hired an assistant, Jeanne Davis. Because her husband was a doctor, Jeanne was familiar with medical terminology and was helpful in researching library books for Rachel.

Rachel's first year of pesticide research ended sadly: Maria Carson died in December 1958. Rachel wrote about her mother to a friend:

> Her love of life and of all living things was her outstanding quality, of which everyone speaks. More than anyone else I know, she embodied Albert Schweitzer's "reverence for life." And while gentle and compassionate, she could fight fiercely against anything she believed wrong, as in our present Crusade [harmful pesticide spraying]! Knowing how she felt about that will help me to return to it soon, and to carry it through to completion.[68]

Exhaustive Investigation

Though Carson had an assistant, the work was slow—but she did not waver. This was a different type of research. Instead of studying tide pools and coral reefs and using Woods Hole laboratories, Carson read mountains of technical material, wrote to pesticide scientists, and researched library books, displaying an almost religious dedication to searching out truths. Carson had hoped to complete the book in 1959. She had written her editor, Paul Brooks:

> In the end I believe you will feel, as I do, that my long and thorough preparation is indispensable to doing an effective job. . . . Now it is as though all the pieces of an extremely complex jigsaw puzzle are at last falling into place.[69]

Carson discovered, however, that she had underestimated the time it would take to complete the research for the book. She was able to spend full days on the work, since Roger was in school. But the nonstop work had a setback. Repeating the medical history of other women in her family, she was now afflicted with arthritis. But something worse was about to interrupt her work.

In spring of 1960 a doctor found two tumors in Rachel's left breast. One turned out to be benign, or free from cancer. She had the suspicious tumor removed. Later, Rachel learned that the surgeon had not been successful in removing all of the cancerous cells. The cancer continued to spread, and she had to undergo twice weekly radiation treatments. The treatments caused Rachel to lose a lot of hair and she had to get a wig.

Even though not in the best of health, Carson continued to work on her book about the dangers of indiscriminate spraying of pesticides.

Rachel Responds to Olga Huckins

After Silent Spring *was published, Rachel wrote to Olga Huckins, the friend whose letter inspired her to write the book. This note appears in* House of Life *by Paul Brooks.*

"I think even you have forgotten, however, that it was not just the copy of your letter to the newspaper but your personal letter to me that started it all. In it you told what had happened and your feelings about the prospect of a new and bigger spraying and begged me to find someone in Washington who could help. It was in the course of finding that 'someone' that I realized that I must write the book."

The treatments also affected her work. Rachel's quiet courage reflected her attitude toward the medical measures being used to treat her disease and its effect on her life: "pretty serious diversion of time and capacity for work. . . . But in the intervals I hope to work hard and productively. Perhaps even more than ever, I am eager to get the book done."[70] At times she was very weak, even bedridden. She worked on her manuscript in bed, listening to spring migrating geese. It broke her heart that she couldn't enjoy the outdoors with eight-year-old Roger.

Although frightened that cancer was still in her body, Carson accepted an invitation to serve on the Natural Resources Committee of the Democratic Advisory Council. Massachusetts senator John F. Kennedy was running for president of the United States at the time. Carson replied:

> My participation will have to be limited, because of temporary health problems and especially because of very heavy writing commitments. However, I do sincerely wish to do all I can.[71]

Carson suggested that the Democratic party include in its platform a statement favoring the control of pollution and the cessation of radioactive contamination of the sea, and chemical poisoning of the environment, coupled with an announced intent to preserve natural wilderness areas. Because of her reputation as a naturalist, Carson was able to secure for environmental issues an important place on the agenda of the Democratic party in a presidential election year.

When Carson was committed to a project, it consumed her life. This overwhelming topic of pesticides would bring new information to the public, and she strived for accuracy. Would her health allow her to complete the project without any more setbacks? Carson certainly was determined to finish what she had started.

Chapter

7 Perseverance

During the four-year period of writing and researching *Silent Spring*, Rachel experienced what she referred to as a "catalog" of illnesses. She shared these in a letter to friends Marjorie Spock and Mary Richards in February 1961:

> I seem always to write of illness and disaster but unfortunately my luck has not changed. Rather severe flu after Thanksgiving and then a persistent intestinal virus early in January apparently lowered my resistance and prepared for the real trouble—a staphylococcus infection that settled in my knees and ankles so that my legs are, and have been for 3 weeks, quite useless. I've been abed all that time, initially of course, quite ill with the infection, but now feeling fairly good if only I could walk! I've had 2 practical nurses all the time, supplementing dear Ida, my housekeeper, who has managed to take beautiful care of me during her hours here.
>
> It has all been very trying for poor Roger, who looks anything but "Jolly" at the moment. Of course our various blizzards have added to the trials of getting people and groceries to the house.[72]

Rachel experienced blindness from an eye infection, but fortunately it lasted only a few weeks. She was also continuing the radiation treatments that had followed her surgery in 1960. Being a private person, she kept the treatments secret from all except immediate family members and close friends. In spite of her illnesses there was a positive side. In March 1961 she wrote to her editor, Paul Brooks:

> About the only good thing I can see in all this experience, is that the long time away from close contact with the book may have given me a broader perspective which I've always struggled for but felt I was not achieving. Now I'm trying to find ways to write it all more simply and perhaps more briefly and with less exhaustive detail.[73]

Writing *Silent Spring*

Having researched and accumulated information from pesticide scientists around the world, from government testimony, and from books, Carson used the material to substantiate her concerns about uncontrolled pesticide spraying.

Carson's main purpose for *Silent Spring* was to explain clearly to the average citizen how uncontrolled pesticide spraying was harmful to all living things. The facts were appalling, distressing, and unwelcome, but Carson was courageous in her goal to educate the public. Carson was correct in her prediction that she would anger pesticide manufacturers as well as farm groups. Farmers insisted that to produce enough crops for the world's increasing population, the use of pesticide sprays was unavoidable. A second purpose of the book was to encourage legislative bodies to write laws to protect our environment.

Carson began *Silent Spring* with a fictitious story in an American town where all creation seemed to exist in harmony. Then an evil spell settled on the community. The shadow of death was everywhere. On farms, chickens, cattle, and families became ill, and some died. In backyards, bird feeding stations were empty. A few birds could be seen, but they trembled violently and couldn't fly. It was a spring without the voices of robins, doves, jays. Apple trees bloomed but were not pollinated because there were no bees; so there would be no fruit. Roadsides were lined with dry, dead vegetation. The streams were lifeless. All the fish had died. This silent world was caused by *people!*

Then Carson concluded the chapter by saying:

> This town does not actually exist, but it might easily have a thousand counterparts in America or elsewhere in the world. I know of no community that has experienced all the misfortunes I describe. Yet every one of these disasters has actually happened somewhere. . . . A grim specter had crept upon us almost unnoticed, and this imagined tragedy may easily become a stark reality we all shall know.[74]

Carson treasures the woods behind her Maine summer cottage.

The book then considered what had silenced voices of spring in many towns in America. Carson explained how living things must interact with their surroundings. Humans in their compulsion to get rid of pests and weeds, have contaminated air, earth, and sea with chemical poisons.

Readers Explode with Anger at Irresponsible Spraying

The famous New York Times *critic Brooks Atkinson discussed one of the* New Yorker *excerpts of* Silent Spring. *The original article appeared in the* Times *on September 11, 1962.*

"Nothing in the field of conservation has provoked such an explosive response as Rachel Carson's articles in the *New Yorker* about the irresponsible use of chemical sprays. . . . Nearly all the letters support her views. Among her earliest and unsought triumphs was a vote of 51 to 7 against the aerial use of insect sprays on Squirrel Island, Me.—a reversal of previous policy ascribed to her articles. . . . Everyone who lives in the country has watched with anger and anxiety the spray trucks, hired by power and telephone companies that hose down the roadside with deadly compounds to kill brush and trees that may reach the wires. They leave what Miss Carson calls 'a sterile and hideous' path of death—skeletons of trees, withered leaves on trees that have not been killed, dead flowers, dead grass. As the years go by, these ugly jungles of death become fire hazards. There is no way of knowing how many birds, animals, bees, worms and insects are also killed. Spraying is cheaper than brush cutting; indiscriminate spraying is the cheapest of all. Also, the most contemptuous to the neighbors and wildlife. . . . Miss Carson's article and the book soon to be published prove the case for ecology, which is also the case for mankind, by stating alarming facts soberly."

This cartoon appeared in the New Yorker *in 1963.*

"Now, don't sell me anything Rachel Carson wouldn't buy"

Sprayers douse insecticides on roadways and bushes in New Jersey.

We have allowed this chemical death rain to alter the natural world.

In chapter after chapter, Carson discussed contamination of surface waters, underground seas, the soil, the sky, plants, and animals. She pointed out that no living thing is immune from contact. She told how uncontrolled spraying—that is, dousing an entire area—is harmful to all life forms.

Carson set out to prove that "chemicals sprayed on croplands, forests, or gardens lie long in the soil and enter into living organisms, passing from one to another in a chain of poisoning and death."[75] Numerous case histories of DDT and pesticide spraying document the occurrence of these disastrous results.

A Plan of Action

Another problem is that if a major pest is eliminated, the population of a minor pest may increase. As an example Carson related the story of the spider mite. In 1956 the U.S. Forest Service sprayed approximately 885,000 acres of western forests with a white cloudy DDT mist to control the spruce budworm. By the following summer, the Douglas firs looked scorched; their burned needles covered the earth. What had happened?

The spider mite, a minor forest pest that was not sensitive to DDT, turned out to have a huge appetite for chlorophyll. Using its sharp mouth parts, the mite pierced and sucked on the outer cells of tree leaves and evergreen needles. In a balanced ecosystem, the natural predators of the spider mite, which include ladybugs,

"Silent Spring" Is Now Noisy Summer

New York Times *reporter John M. Lee wrote about the pesticide industry's very angry response to the facts Carson presented in* Silent Spring. *This excerpt from a front-page article published on July 22, 1962, describes some reactions to the* New Yorker *series.*

"The $300,000,000 pesticides industry has been highly irritated by a quiet woman author whose previous works on science have been praised for the beauty and precision of the writing. . . . The men who make the pesticides are crying foul. 'Crass commercialism or idealistic flag waving,' scoffs one industrial toxicologist. 'We are aghast,' says another. 'Our members are raising hell,' reports a trade association. Some agricultural chemicals concerns have set their scientists to analyzing Miss Carson's work, line by line. Other companies are preparing briefs defending the use of their products. Meetings have been held in Washington and New York. Statements are being drafted and counter-attacks plotted. A drowsy midsummer has suddenly been enlivened by the greatest uproar in the pesticides industry since the cranberry scare of 1959. . . . The industry feels that [Carson] has presented a one-sided case and has chosen to ignore the enormous benefits in increased food production and decreased incidence of disease that have accrued from the development and use of modern pesticides. The pesticides industry is annoyed also at the implications that the industry itself has not been alert and concerned in its recognition of the problems that accompany pesticide use. . . . Tom K. Smith, Monsanto Chemical Company, said the articles [in the *New Yorker*] suggested that government officials and private and industrial scientists were either not as well informed on pesticide problems as Miss Carson, not professionally competent to evaluate possible hazards, or else remiss in their obligations to society."

gall midges, and pirate bugs, can control the tiny pests. In the western forests, however, all these predators were killed by the DDT. Without enemies, then, the spider mite increased its egg production threefold, and soon this booming population destroyed the beautiful green forest.

Carson offered several suggestions for a plan of action to get off this disastrous road of pesticide spraying. She advised a combined effort: control the aerial spraying of pesticides; use biological control, including insect sterilization; and develop synthetic insect lures or attractants called pheromones. She didn't suggest stopping all spraying, but rather advocated the discriminating use of the sprays. To show scientific responsibility, Carson concluded the book with a fifty-five-page appendix of sources.

Publication and Reaction

Carson completed writing *Silent Spring* in early 1962, and her agent, Marie Rodell, sent the manuscript to Houghton Mifflin and to the *New Yorker*, which had expressed interest in printing excerpts from the book.

Carson didn't have to wait long for a reaction to her work. In less than a week, *New Yorker* editor William Shawn telephoned to say that he was very impressed with Carson's information. He was also appalled by her findings. He couldn't wait to print her facts.

After the phone call from Shawn, Rachel put the Beethoven violin concerto on her record player and wrote to Dorothy Freeman, her Maine neighbor and good friend:

In Huntington Park, California, an apple tree is sprayed with malathion.

Carson's Book Is One-Sided!

On September 14, 1962, the New York Times *reported one establishment spokesman's attack on* Silent Spring.

"A public frame of mind 'bordering on hysteria' can be generated by 'one-sided' books such as that just written by Rachel Carson, it was charged today by Dr. C. Glen King, head of the Nutrition Foundation. . . . Dr. King argued that the United States could not maintain an adequate food supply for its population without agricultural chemicals. True, he said, there have been tragic accidents in the use of such chemicals, as described extensively in Miss Carson's book on pesticides. However he said, to concentrate on such mishaps is like writing an account of automotive transport that gleans nation-wide records of accidents in which people are maimed, 'pretending all this happened in one community at one time.' This, he asserted, 'is exactly what *Silent Spring* has done.'"

Suddenly the tension of four years was broken, and I let the tears come. I think I let you see last summer what my deeper feelings are about this when I said I could never again listen happily to a thrush song if I had not done all I could. And last night the thoughts of all the birds and other creatures and all the loveliness that is in nature came to me with such a surge of deep happiness that now I had done what I could—I had been able to complete it—now it had its own life.[76]

The June 16, 1962, issue of the *New Yorker,* carried Part One of a fifty-thousand-word condensation of *Silent Spring.* Two more weekly installments followed. The book itself would not be out until late September. Immediately letters poured in from coast to coast. Carson's post office box in Maine overflowed daily. Letters were written by people all across the country to Congress, to the Public Health Service, to the departments of agriculture and the interior, to the Food and Drug Administration, and to local agencies. Hundreds of editorials and newspaper columns were written about *Silent Spring.* Most articles were supportive. The public demanded that government take action. People were outraged by the betrayal of chemical companies and government for allowing uncontrolled pesticide spraying.

After reading the excerpts in the *New Yorker,* Velsicol Chemical Company wrote Houghton Mifflin, in an attempt to persuade the respected Boston firm to halt

Chemists Debate Pesticides Book

In another article in the September 14, 1962, New York Times, *Walter Sullivan reported chemical industry representatives' belief that* Silent Spring *might deter the development of new and better pesticides.*

"Spokesmen for the pesticide industry and the Government disputed today [*Silent Spring*'s] contention that pesticides seriously threaten life on earth. . . . Industry representatives said today that Miss Carson's book might slacken the pace of pesticide development. If, they said, there is danger that the public will turn against the use of chemicals to kill weeds, insects, and other pests, industry will not want to spend large sums to seek better substances for these purposes. . . . Despite their distress over *Silent Spring*, the industry men conceded that most of the facts in it were correct. They objected, however, to the use of these facts to argue that chemical contamination of the environment ranks with nuclear war in threatening 'the extinction of mankind.' "

publication of the book. Threatening a lawsuit, Velsicol accused Carson of presenting inaccurate information on chlordane, a pesticide they manufacture. After Carson's information was verified and found accurate, the suit was dropped.

The book was also discussed in Congress. At a news conference, a reporter addressed President Kennedy:

> "There appears to be growing concern among scientists as to the possibility of dangerous, long-range side effects from the widespread use of DDT and other pesticides. Have you considered asking the Department of Agriculture or the Public Health Service to take a closer look at this?" The president answered: "Yes . . . particularly, since Miss Carson's book . . . they are examining the matter."[77]

Stabs at *Silent Spring*

After *Silent Spring* was published in September 1962, attacks on Carson and the book increased. The National Agricultural Chemicals Association spent $250,000 on a booklet to discredit Carson's data. Because her data were factual, however, the plan backfired and worked to the advantage of *Silent Spring* sales. Other organizations, as well as publications that received income from chemical industry advertisements, joined in belittling *Silent Spring*.

Some scientists criticizing Carson's work were on the payrolls of chemical companies. Other critics had received grants for research from the companies they were defending. Many negative commentaries came from people who feared losing their jobs.

Carson was labeled a hysterical woman, a nature nut, a middle-aged nervous Nellie. She was the subject of many cartoons across the nation. The *New York Times* had headlines such as

> "SILENT SPRING" IS NOW NOISY SUMMER.
>
> PESTICIDES INDUSTRY UP IN ARMS OVER A NEW BOOK.
>
> RACHEL CARSON STIRS CONFLICT—PRODUCERS ARE CRYING "FOUL."[78]

Carson's work also drew praise. The impact of *Silent Spring* was compared with that of another book, *Uncle Tom's Cabin* by Harriet Beecher Stowe. A century earlier, *Uncle Tom's Cabin* had exposed the evils of slavery. *Silent Spring* was exposing the dangers of tampering with our environment.

The reviewer for the *New York Times* said:

> In her new book [Carson] tries to scare the living daylights out of us and, in large measure, succeeds. Her work tingles with anger, outrage, and protest. It is a 20th-century *Uncle Tom's Cabin*. . . . The dangers that Miss Carson recounts so vividly are overstated, but they are real. No householder who has read her book will ever reach again for an insecticide or weed killer without second thoughts. The neglected science of ecology, dealing with the interdependence of all forms of life is dealt with magnificently in some chapters.[79]

The whirlwind of denouncement versus approval continued for eleven months.

The *Saturday Review* reported:

> In the face of all this furor Rachel Carson remains immaculately calm, detached, self-sure. . . . Rachel Carson, at fifty-six, has become what she dreaded most: a controversial celebrity.[80]

The incredible sales of half a million hardcover copies of *Silent Spring* were proof that Carson had achieved what she had set out to do: to alert people about the dangers of irresponsible pesticide spraying. The book was translated into twenty-two languages and sold worldwide. No matter what language, the message was the same: we must be careful what we do to the earth.

Carson's work became the subject of many cartoons.

"Just say the blow was inflicted by a blunt instrument."

Gordon Brooks in *Yankee* magazine, May, 1963

Rachel Carson holds a copy of Silent Spring *inside her home in Silver Spring, Maryland.*

A Showdown on Television

Carson's dedication to the planet kept her determined to go on. Even though cancer was causing her health to deteriorate rapidly, Carson agreed to be a guest on the television program *CBS Reports.* A segment entitled "The Silent Spring of Rachel Carson" was planned as a showdown between Carson and some of her critics. During the taping Carson was nervous, but she wanted to use this opportunity to support her facts before millions of viewers so that people could judge for themselves. The show aired on April 3, 1963. Carson stirred viewers with her calm, soft-spoken, assured manner and unshakable knowledge of her subject.

Dr. Robert White-Stevens, a research executive for the American Cyanamid Company, also appeared on the show to discredit Carson's facts or downplay their significance. He had campaigned tirelessly against Carson and her ideas, giving a total of twenty-eight speeches.

Three government spokesmen, the secretary of agriculture, the chief of the Public Health Service, and the commissioner of the Food and Drug Administration, appeared as well. During the discussion, each one defended the use of pesticides as not damaging to human health or to crops. However, the government officials agreed that Carson knew what she was talking about, that the dangers were real and needed more investigating, and that stricter controls on chemical use were called for. The showdown went dramatically in Carson's favor. Carson was pleased with the program when she and ten-year-old Roger watched it at home in Silver Spring.

Effects of *Silent Spring*

So persuasive were the facts in *Silent Spring* that by the end of 1962 more than forty bills regulating pesticides had been introduced into state legislatures.

Federal government agencies were caught in the middle. The Department of Agriculture had encouraged the use of pesticides because they helped farmers grow bigger, more profitable crops. The Public Health Service was happy that overnight, in a given area, cheap materials could wipe out the agents that carry sleeping sickness and malaria. The Food and Drug Administration couldn't afford to enforce regulation designed to prevent the sale or use of foods with high pesticide content. However, the Department of the Interior challenged the safety of certain chemicals. Land and water animals such as fish, birds, and clams, which were their responsibility, were visible subjects of poisons. Top scientists appointed by President Kennedy agreed with Rachel's findings and now had to set regulations.

Shortly after the book was published, President Kennedy responded to Carson's message and set up a special panel. Within the President's Science Advisory

Silent Spring Shocks the World

In the opening chapter of Silent Spring, *Rachel Carson offers a grim description of misfortunes that have occurred in towns across the world.*

"A strange blight crept over the area and everything began to change . . . mysterious maladies swept the flocks of chickens; the cattle and sheep sickened and died. . . . The farmers spoke of much illness among their families. . . . There was a strange stillness . . . birds . . . trembled violently and could not fly . . . on the farms the hens brooded, but no chicks hatched. . . . The apple trees were coming into bloom but no bees droned among the blossoms, so there was no pollination and there would be no fruit. . . . The roadsides, once so attractive, were now lined with browned and withered vegetation as though swept by fire. These, too, were silent, deserted by all living things. Even the streams were now lifeless. . . . No witchcraft, no enemy action had silenced the rebirth of new life in this stricken world. The people had done it themselves."

Committee (PSAC), this panel, under the direction of Dr. Jerome B. Weisner, was formed to study the use and control of pesticides. The group considered both the benefits and the dangers. In January 1963 Carson testified before a committee and so did representatives of the chemical industry.

Carson's Facts Pass the Test

On May 15, 1963, the PSAC made its final report public. It had decided that *Silent Spring* was indeed factual. As a result, the government would begin to monitor and control pesticide use. Human safety would be a consideration. The forty-three-page report to the president strongly supported *Silent Spring* in its scientific correctness and public importance, but its authors also wanted to avoid being perceived as "antichemical":

> The use of pesticides must be continued. . . . On the other hand it has now become clear that . . . while they destroy harmful insects and plants, pesticides may also be toxic to beneficial plants and animals, including man.[81]

Following the PSAC report, the Columbia Broadcasting System did a follow-up on pesticides and the committee's findings. Correspondent Eric Sevareid interviewed Rachel for the program, which he ended with this comment:

> Her book and this report deal with the same facts, the same issues. The first was a cry of alarm from a quietly passionate woman. The second is a sober warning by dispassionate judges. . . . Miss Carson had two immediate aims. One was to alert the public; the second, to build a fire under the government.[82]

Because of the PSAC's support, many publications reversed their editorial stance.

For the next two years, a Senate subcommittee on government operations investigated pollutions, beginning with chemical pesticides. Carson was invited to speak to the subcommittee several times.

In June 1963 Carson testified before a new Senate committee headed by Abraham Ribicoff of Connecticut, formed to study environmental hazards and the control of pesticides. Carson ended her testimony with the following recommendations: (1) That aerial spraying of pesticides be brought under strict control. (2) That the

Six weeks after the initial TV show, Eric Sevareid does a follow-up interview for CBS in Carson's home. The support of the PSAC gave credibility to her well-researched facts.

On June 4, 1963, Carson testified before the Senate Government Operations Subcommittee.

committee give its support to new programs of medical research and education in the field of pesticides. (3) That legislation be enacted to restrict the sale and use of pesticides to those capable of understanding the accompanying hazards. (4) That the authority to oversee registration and labeling of chemicals be assigned to the Department of the Interior. (5) That new pesticides be approved only when no existing chemical or other method would do the job. (6) That biological controls be used, if possible. How soon would the government act on these recommendations?

Though not in the best of health, Carson promoted her book as much as she could. She granted magazine and newspaper interviews. She attended luncheons in her honor and autographed copies of her book. Carson's calendar was filled with visits to many cities including New York, Cleveland, Washington, D.C., and Richmond.

We Must Learn to Live with Insects

Carson states in Silent Spring *that humans need to share the planet with other species.*

"Through all these new, imaginative, and creative approaches to the problem of sharing our earth with other creatures there runs a constant theme, the awareness that we are dealing with life—with living populations and all their pressures and counterpressures, their surges and recessions. Only by taking account of such life forces and by cautiously seeking to guide them into channels favorable to ourselves can we hope to achieve a reasonable accommodation between the insect hordes and ourselves."

Carson received numerous awards and honors for her dedication to the environment. She was inducted into the American Academy of Arts and Letters, a prestigious group of writers, artists, and musicians. This honor made her one of only four women out of a membership of fifty. She was the first woman to receive the Audubon Society's highest award for conservation achievement, the coveted Audubon Medal.

Carson's most prized award for *Silent Spring* was the Schweitzer Medal of the Animal Welfare Institute. In accepting she said:

Because of her persistence and dedication to saving the environment, Rachel Carson has been called the founder of today's ecology movement.

> I can think of no award that would have more meaning for me or that would touch me more deeply than this one, coupled as it is with the name of Albert Schweitzer. [He] has told us that we are not being truly civilized if we concern ourselves only with the relation of man to man. What is important is the relation of man to all life.[83]

As the cancer progressed to her bones and radiation treatments left her weary, Carson sent friends in her place to accept awards and give speeches. She was saddened to have to pass up many invitations to travel to foreign countries.

The Joy of Nature Never Stops

Rachel's enthusiasm for nature's gifts spread even to children she met on a walk near her Maryland home:

> Did you ever collect frog eggs down here? Take your microscope out in the sun and see them develop right after they've been laid. And if you have field glasses, go out when the moon is full. If you wait you'll see migrating birds high up in the sky flying.[84]

In spring of 1963, Rachel suffered a nonfatal heart attack. She spent that summer recuperating at her Maine seaside cottage, with Roger and a cat at her side. She passed many hours on her deck, using binoculars to observe tiny creatures, songbirds, and swooping gulls. She enjoyed sunrises and sunsets, the stars, the surging tides, and the changing autumn colors. Rachel and her neighbor Dorothy Freeman had many pleasant picnic conversations while enjoying nature's wonders, including a fall migration of monarch butterflies.

Later, back in Maryland, Rachel wrote to Dorothy about her memory of the monarchs:

> We talked a little about their life history. Did they return? We thought not; for most, at least, this was the closing journey of their lives. . . . It had been a happy spectacle. For ourselves, the thought is the same: when that intangible cycle has run its course, it is a natural and not unhappy thing that a life comes to its end.[85]

Rachel was preparing for her own death.

In the fall, Carson accepted an invitation to speak at the Kaiser Medical Center in San Francisco. Marie Rodell accompanied her. While in California, even though confined to a wheelchair, Carson couldn't pass up a visit to the famous Muir Woods, a national monument known for its grove of redwood trees.

Rachel spent the first months of 1964 in pain. She had surgery in February. In early April, Dorothy Freeman came to visit. Rachel's last wish was to be wheeled from room to room through her Silver Spring home to look at all the things that pleased her: books, a favorite tablecloth, rose bushes visible from the living-room window. A few days later, on April 14, 1964, Rachel died at the age of fifty-six of cancer and heart disease.

Rachel relishes the ocean breezes on the porch of her cottage in Maine.

As her epitaph, the *Saturday Review* printed these lines of the poet John Keats:

> Beauty is truth,
> Truth beauty,—
> That is all ye know on earth,
> and all ye need to know.[86]

Chapter

8 Today's World

Rachel Carson's last years were spent trying to protect nature from humanity and also defending humanity from its own acts. She was not afraid to stand by her belief in the right of all living things to a healthy environment. Through her book *Silent Spring,* Carson started the environmental movement, making ecology, the relationship between living organisms and their environment, a well-known concept. At a symposium in 1992, author Ann Cottrell Free, who had been a friend of Rachel Carson, said:

> Please let us not forget our relationship with all that lives. Remember the meaning of ecology: we live in the house of life and all the rooms connect.[87]

In writing *Silent Spring,* Carson succeeded in making a book about death a celebration of life.

Long-Term Effects of *Silent Spring*

Rachel Carson's friend Shirley Briggs states in a twenty-fifth anniversary supplement of *Silent Spring*:

> Into the fray [fight] have come the many ordinary people . . . who see both their own lives and the future of their children at stake, and who have insisted that the direction of policy and practices be changed. It is through these people and the influential government officials whom Rachel Carson reached directly through the book that concrete changes have been made.[88]

Today, concern for the environment is almost considered a form of etiquette.

A 1970 cartoon commemorates Rachel Carson.

Rachel Carson played a part in that thinking. Environmental agencies have sprung up around the world to protect the earth. Goals for responsible energy use, the sustainment of agriculture programs, the protection of forests, and the abatement of pollution are being actively addressed. All these concerns reflect Rachel Carson's battle to compel humans to respect and protect the web of life. Carson's greatest contribution is having inspired so many people to work on behalf of the environment.

Since Carson's death in 1964, dozens of federal laws and hundreds of state laws have been passed to protect our environment. Many government agencies have been created to guard against the pollution of water, air, and soil.

In 1970, fulfilling a request of Rachel Carson at the Senate hearings seven years earlier, the U.S. Environmental Protection Agency(EPA) was formed. One of the functions of this governmental board was to monitor chemicals that affect the environment. An article in the *EPA Journal* referred to the agency as "the extended shadow of Rachel Carson"[89] which, no doubt, would have pleased her. The U.S. EPA is now the largest environmental agency in the world.

Safety standards now require new pesticides to be registered. The EPA reviews the chemicals by using data about their effects on soil, water, wildlife, and humans. In response to *Silent Spring*, the federal government also checks pesticide levels in foods to make sure they are within safe

Reflections from Roger Christie

After Rachel's death, Paul Brooks and his wife welcomed Roger Christie into their family. In a 1993 PBS American Experience *television program entitled "Rachel Carson's* Silent Spring,*" Roger Christie, aged forty-nine, reflected on his relationship with the great-aunt who had adopted him.*

"I never forgot that I had another mother who was a real mother, but Rachel was my mother too, after my mother died. We would spend a lot of time on the beach, obviously. She would find something interesting and call me over, 'Look at this!' She was a great one for getting down and peering under the rocks. She was very concerned about keeping alive a sense of wonder in children. It was more imparting a philosophy, a way of looking at things. . . . I was probably eleven when *Silent Spring* was actually published, so things were very black and white to me. Rachel was the good guy and anybody that was attacking her wore the black hats. We collected all the editorial cartoons and that sort of thing and there was a whole lot of commotion. The CBS people came and did an interview at our house in Maryland."

The peregrine falcon was one of the large birds faced with extinction in the 1960s due to DDT.

limits. In addition, industry has been encouraged to develop less persistent pesticides. Concerned farmers are also using lower amounts of pesticides plus natural methods of pest control.

Integrated Pest Management

Today it is understood that chemical pesticides are not all bad. Used with care, they help increase food production. Because the world's population is increasing, larger food harvests are necessary. And this means that crop growers still must fight pests.

Farmers are encouraged to plant pest-resistant crops and to rotate crops frequently to different fields while using only moderate spraying. The use of a combination of methods to control crop pests is called integrated pest management (IPM). IPM also makes use of natural predators and pheromones, the synthetic chemical attractants Carson had promoted as a means of weaning agriculture away from dangerous chemicals.

IPM requires continuous monitoring by experienced people with detailed knowledge of pests, crops, and localities. According to the American Chemical Society:

> Without pesticides, it is estimated that pests would destroy thirty percent of our agricultural foods and that could mean economic and human disaster of starvation, especially for developing countries.[90]

DDT

In 1972 the EPA severely restricted the nationwide sale and use of DDT. And in 1980 DDT use was totally eliminated in the United States and most other countries of the world. However, a few pesticide manufacturers continue to manufacture and sell DDT to underdeveloped countries, including Mexico. All humans pay a price for the unrestricted use of pesticides wherever they are used, because pesticides stay in the environment for ten to thirty years; they dissolve slowly, and can move out of the sprayed area into the surrounding environment. Imported food is another source of danger.

What happened to the areas where robins had been silenced by DDT, as described in *Silent Spring*? Have the birds returned, or are they still absent? In *Silent Spring—The View from 1987*, Shirley Briggs wrote:

> Some gradual silencing of spring has been noted in many places. In my suburban neighborhood the difference is apparent. Dawn once brought the sound of widening circles of robin song, from those nearby out to the limit of audibility. I am lucky now to hear one robin. How much can we

blame DDT, and how much of this loss of song from robins and other once dependable bird species comes from the continuing application of even more lethal chemicals?[91]

In the time since DDT was banned in the United States, some endangered species of large birds have begun to recover, namely , the bald eagle, the brown pelican, and the peregrine falcon. These three species were facing extinction in the 1960s. DDT had caused the birds to produce thin-shelled eggs and deformed chicks. After DDT was restricted, peregrine falcons were hand-raised by scientists to save the species. In 1979 a healthy peregrine falcon named Rachel, in Carson's honor, was released in Washington, D.C., an event the lifelong bird-watcher would have cherished.

Humans are constantly exposed to pesticides. DDT is stored in fatty tissues of fish, poultry, cows, and pigs. It begins its journey up the food chain when an animal eats contaminated plants or drinks DDT-polluted water. The concentration of DDT in fatty tissue increases at each level of the food chain. DDT is not quickly eliminated from fatty tissue—not even in the human body. According to Carson's research, DDT is also responsible for causing blood disorders such as leukemia and some other forms of cancer.

Rachel Carson suggested the application of biological controls to replace heavy dousing with pesticides. In one well-known example, natural enemies were used to combat mosquitoes. Heavy rains had resulted in standing water everywhere in Los Angeles. Mosquitoes, which lay their eggs in water, had deposited them in backyard ponds, rain barrels, horse troughs, and lakes. At the suggestion of public health officials, predator "mosquito fish" were made available to local residents at no charge. These tiny, guppylike fish thrive by eating wiggly mosquito larvae. Used since 1952, the mosquito fish have been able to control specific diseases carried by mosquitoes.

Disease-carrying mosquitoes are controlled naturally by the mosquito fish (left), which thrives on the insects' larvae. Southeast Mosquito Abatement District workers haul in a mosquito-fish catch for distribution.

Another destructive pest is the Mediterranean fruit fly. In the 1970s, when the fly was destroying more than 250 kinds of fruits and vegetables in California, the pesticide malathion was sprayed from airplanes. Now, however, the California Department of Food & Agriculture uses several methods of Medfly control. In one combined approach, the chemically synthesized scent of female insects is used to lure males into traps, and sterilized male insects are released into the target area.

When a Medfly is discovered in a trap or inspection system, measures such as ground malathion spraying, stripping the infested trees of their fruit, or releasing hordes of sterilized flies are instituted immediately. This is an example of a combination of natural control with reduced and regulated chemical spraying. Unfortunately, aerial malathion spraying was used again in 1994 against the Medfly.

Tributes to Rachel Carson

Before Carson died, she discussed with friends and colleagues the possibility of some sort of committee to dispense to the public information about pesticides and chemical contamination. After her death in 1964 the Rachel Carson Council was established in Chevy Chase, Maryland. National and regional groups now work with this organization to educate the public.

In 1970 a portion of the Maine coast was named the Rachel Carson National Wildlife Refuge. Ten years later, President Jimmy Carter awarded Carson, posthumously, the highest government civilian award. Handing the Presidential Medal of Freedom to Carson's adopted son, Roger, President Carter said:

> Never silent herself in the face of destructive trends, Rachel Carson fed a

About forty-five miles of the southern Maine coast have been preserved as a wildlife refuge in tribute to Carson's memory. Meandering tidal creeks wander through a salt marsh on a section of the walking trail (right).

Are Humans Pests?

In her book Pesticides, *Sally Lee points to human responsibility for the misuse of substances not found in nature but, rather, developed by people.*

"If pests are judged by the amount of damage they do to our environment, then the world's most dangerous pests are humans. It was through human ingenuity that pesticides were first developed. Human carelessness allowed these chemicals to threaten the environment. Now it is time for human ingenuity to come up with ways for pest control measures and the environment to work together. We must accept the fact that we will never gain control over insects. As a wise scientist has said, 'The object of our game with nature is not to win, but to keep on playing.' "

spring of awareness across America and beyond. A biologist with a gentle, clear voice, she welcomed her audiences to her love of the sea, while with an equally clear determined voice she warned Americans of the dangers human beings pose for their own environment. Always concerned, always eloquent, she created a tide of environmental consciousness that has not ebbed.[92]

Both Carson's childhood home in Springdale, Pennsylvania, and her final home in Silver Spring, Maryland, have been designated National Historic Landmarks.

In April 1993 a Rachel Carson Graduate Fellowship was announced by the Virginia Polytechnic Institute and State University in association with the Rachel Carson Council. It supports projects in the study of environmental poisons, conservation education, and nongame wildlife management.

In 1987, twenty-five years after the publication of *Silent Spring*, Jay D. Hair, executive vice president of the National Wildlife Federation, talked about what Rachel Carson has meant to the world:

> Rachel Carson's works, especially *Silent Spring*, are so eloquent, so carefully researched, and so prophetic that they have moved thousands of people from apathy to action.[93]

Carson had no idea of the impact of her research on future generations. She could only hope her concerns for the environment would be taken up by others. Asked how Rachel Carson would feel about the state of the environment today, her editor Paul Brooks wrote in September 1993:

> Although pesticide changes have been slow Carson would have been impressed—perhaps astonished—at the influence she has had worldwide.[94]

Notes

Chapter 1: Rural Heaven

1. Marty Jezer, *Rachel Carson.* New York: Chelsea House, 1988.
2. Quoted in Paul Brooks, *The House of Life: Rachel Carson at Work.* Boston: Houghton Mifflin, 1989.
3. Quoted in Brooks, *House of Life.*
4. Quoted in Brooks, *House of Life.*
5. Quoted in Brooks, *House of Life.*
6. Quoted in Philip Sterling, *Sea and Earth: The Life of Rachel Carson.* New York: Crowell, 1970.
7. Quoted in Brooks, *House of Life.*
8. Quoted in Brooks, *House of Life.*

Chapter 2: College Years Lure Rachel to Nature

9. Quoted in Sterling, *Sea and Earth.*
10. Quoted in Sterling, *Sea and Earth.*
11. Quoted in Brooks, *House of Life.*
12. Quoted in Sterling, *Sea and Earth.*
13. Brooks, *House of Life.*
14. Quoted in Carol B. Gartner, *Rachel Carson.* New York: Ungar, 1983.
15. Quoted in Sterling, *Sea and Earth.*
16. Quoted in Sterling, *Sea and Earth.*
17. Quoted in Doris Faber and Harold Faber, *Nature and the Environment, Great Lives.* New York: Scribner's, 1991.
18. Quoted in Kathleen V. Kudlinski, *Rachel Carson, Pioneer of Ecology.* New York: Viking Kestrel, 1988.

Chapter 3: The Magic of the Seas

19. Quoted in Sterling, *Sea and Earth.*
20. Quoted in Sterling, *Sea and Earth.*
21. Quoted in Brooks, *House of Life.*
22. Quoted in Brooks, *House of Life.*
23. Quoted in Brooks, *House of Life.*
24. Quoted in Gartner, *Rachel Carson.*
25. Quoted in Faber and Faber, *Nature and the Environment.*
26. Quoted in Brooks, *House of Life.*

Chapter 4: Work and Leisure Activities Mesh

27. Quoted in Sterling, *Sea and Earth.*
28. Quoted in Sterling, *Sea and Earth.*
29. Rachel L. Carson, *Under the Sea-Wind,* 50th anniversary edition. New York: Truman Talley Books/Dutton, 1991.
30. Quoted in Brooks, *House of Life.*
31. Quoted in Sterling, *Sea and Earth.*
32. Quoted in Brooks, *House of Life.*
33. Quoted in Sterling, *Sea and Earth.*
34. Quoted in Brooks, *House of Life.*
35. Quoted in Brooks, *House of Life.*
36. Quoted in Sterling, *Sea and Earth.*
37. Quoted in Brooks, *House of Life.*
38. Quoted in Judith Harlan, *Sounding the Alarm—A Biography of Rachel Carson.* Minneapolis, MN: Dillon Press, 1989.
39. Quoted in Jezer, *Rachel Carson.*
40. Quoted in Jezer, *Rachel Carson.*
41. Quoted in Sterling, *Sea and Earth.*
42. Quoted in Brooks, *House of Life.*
43. Quoted in Brooks, *House of Life.*

Chapter 5: Wondrous Senses

44. Rachel Carson, *The Sea Around Us,* edition for young readers. New York: Golden Press, 1958.
45. Carson, *The Sea Around Us.*
46. Austin H. Clark, "From the Beginning of the World," *Saturday Review of Literature,* July 7, 1951.

47. Quoted in Brooks, *House of Life.*
48. Quoted in Brooks, *House of Life.*
49. Quoted in Sterling, *Sea and Earth.*
50. Quoted in Brooks, *House of Life.*
51. Quoted in Brooks, *House of Life.*
52. Quoted in Sterling, *Sea and Earth.*
53. Quoted in Sterling, *Sea and Earth.*
54. Rachel Carson, *The Edge of the Sea.* Boston: Houghton Mifflin, 1955.
55. Carson, *The Edge of the Sea.*
56. Carson, *The Edge of the Sea.*
57. Carson, *The Edge of the Sea.*
58. Rachel Carson, *The Sense of Wonder.* New York: Harper & Row, 1965.
59. Quoted in Brooks, *House of Life.*

Chapter 6: Songbirds Are Silenced

60. Quoted in Brooks, *House of Life.*
61. Quoted in Brooks, *House of Life.*
62. Quoted in Brooks, *House of Life.*
63. Quoted in Brooks, *House of Life.*
64. Quoted in Brooks, *House of Life.*
65. Quoted in Brooks, *House of Life.*
66. Quoted in Jezer, *Rachel Carson.*
67. Quoted in Brooks, *House of Life.*
68. Quoted in Brooks, *House of Life.*
69. Quoted in Gartner, *Rachel Carson.*
70. Quoted in Brooks, *House of Life.*
71. Quoted in Brooks, *House of Life.*

Chapter 7: Perseverance

72. Quoted in Brooks, *House of Life.*
73. Quoted in Brooks, *House of Life.*
74. Rachel Carson, *Silent Spring.* Boston: Houghton Mifflin, 1962.
75. Ann Cottrell Free, *Since Silent Spring: Our Debt to Albert Schweitzer & Rachel Carson.* Washington, DC: Flying Fox Press, 1992.
76. Quoted in Harlan, *Sounding the Alarm.*
77. Quoted in Marjorie Hunter, "U.S. Sets Up Panel to Review the Side Effects of Pesticides," *New York Times,* August 31, 1962.
78. Quoted in Sterling, *Sea and Earth.*
79. Walter Sullivan, "Books of the Times," *New York Times,* September 27, 1962.
80. Loren Eiseley, "Using a Plague to Fight a Plague," *Saturday Review,* September 29, 1962.
81. Quoted in Sterling, *Sea and Earth.*
82. Quoted in Sterling, *Sea and Earth.*
83. Quoted in Harlan, *Sounding the Alarm.*
84. Quoted in "Gentle Storm Center: Calm Appraisal of *Silent Spring,*" *Life,* October 12, 1962.
85. Quoted in Harlan, *Sounding the Alarm.*
86. Quoted in Stewart L. Udall, "The Legacy of Rachel Carson," *Saturday Review,* May 16, 1964.

Chapter 8: Today's World

87. Free, *Since Silent Spring.*
88. Shirley A. Briggs, *Silent Spring—The View from 1987.* Chevy Chase, MD: Rachel Carson Council, 1987.
89. John Henricksson, *Rachel Carson: The Environmental Movement.* Brookfield, CT: New Directions, Millbrook Press, 1991.
90. C.F. Wilkinson, "The Science and Politics of Pesticides," in *Silent Spring Revisited.* Washington, DC: American Chemical Society, 1987.
91. Briggs, *The View from 1987.*
92. Quoted in Faber and Faber, *Nature and the Environment.*
93. Quoted in Harlan, *Sounding the Alarm.*
94. Paul Brooks, letter to author, Judith Presnall, September 1, 1993.

For Further Reading

Rachel Carson, *The Sea Around Us.* New York: Golden Press, 1958. This special edition for young readers describes the layers of the sea and its inhabitants.

Rachel Carson, *The Sense of Wonder.* New York: Harper & Row, 1965. This information first appeared in a 1956 *Woman's Home Companion* article, "Help Your Child to Wonder."

Judith Harlan, *Sounding the Alarm—A Biography of Rachel Carson.* Minneapolis, MN: Dillon Press, 1989. Traces the life and achievements of the biologist who wrote about the sea and the dangers of pesticides.

John Henricksson, *Rachel Carson: The Environmental Movement.* Brookfield, CT: New Directions, Millbrook Press, 1991. A biography of Rachel Carson focusing on her exposure of pesticide pollution and her legacy as founder of the environmental movement.

Marty Jezer, *Rachel Carson.* New York: Chelsea House, 1988. A biography of the marine biologist whose writings stressed the interrelation of all living things and the dependence of human welfare on natural processes.

Kathleen V. Kudlinski, *Rachel Carson, Pioneer of Ecology.* New York: Viking Kestrel, 1988. An account of how one gifted scientist and writer, Rachel Carson, changed the way people look at their planet.

Catherine Reef, *Rachel Carson: The Wonder of Nature.* Frederick, MD: Twenty-First Century Books, 1992. Follows the life of the biologist and conservationist, known for her writing on the environment.

Elizabeth Ring, *Rachel Carson: Caring for the Earth.* Brookfield, CT: Millbrook Press, 1992. A biography of the biologist focusing on her childhood, the environment, and the importance of her book, *Silent Spring.*

Philip Sterling, *Sea and Earth: The Life of Rachel Carson.* New York: Crowell, 1970. Drawing much of the story from recollections of friends, the biographer portrays Rachel's life in an easy-to-read format.

Eve Stwertka, *Rachel Carson.* New York: Franklin Watts, 1991. Describes the life and studies of Rachel Carson, highlighting her writing and activities to save the environment.

Ginger Wadsworth, *Rachel Carson, Voice for the Earth.* Minneapolis, MN: Lerner, 1992. Describes the life and work of the biologist and writer who helped initiate the environmental movement.

Wendy Wareham, "Rachel Carson's Early Years," *Carnegie Magazine,* November/December 1986. An article researched and written by a lifetime resident of Springdale, Pennsylvania, who talked to Carson's college friend, Dorothy Thompson Seif, and the Historical Committee of the Rachel Carson Homestead Association, which conducted interviews with Springdale residents who knew the Carsons.

Works Consulted

Books

Shirley A. Briggs, *Silent Spring—The View from 1987.* Chevy Chase, MD: Rachel Carson Council, 1987. This pamphlet was supposed to be an Afterword chapter for the twenty-fifth anniversary edition of *Silent Spring.* Refused by the publisher because it was insufficiently optimistic and too critical of the pesticide industry, the material has been made available independently.

Paul Brooks, *The House of Life: Rachel Carson at Work.* Boston: Houghton Mifflin, 1989. This biography contains quotations and letters and other previously unpublished writings.

Rachel Carson, *The Edge of the Sea.* Boston: Houghton Mifflin, 1955. This best-selling book describes the surf, currents, tides, and waters of the sea, as well as a rocky coast, sand beaches, and the world of coral reefs.

Rachel Carson, *Silent Spring.* Boston: Houghton Mifflin, 1962. The author educates the world about the danger of pesticide use.

Rachel L. Carson, *Under the Sea-Wind,* 50th anniversary edition. New York: Truman Talley Books/Dutton, 1991. Carson's first book is an introduction to winds and ocean currents. The reader follows the adventures of Scomber, a mackerel, Ookpik, a snowy owl, and other animals whose lives are intimately tied to the sea.

Doris Faber and Harold Faber, *Nature and the Environment, Great Lives.* New York: Scribner's, 1991. Twenty-five naturalists, conservationists, and environmentalists are described.

Ann Cottrell Free, *Since Silent Spring: Our Debt to Albert Schweitzer & Rachel Carson.* Washington, DC: Flying Fox Press, 1992. A reprint of an address given to a symposium held in New York in August 1992.

Carol B. Gartner, *Rachel Carson.* New York: Ungar, 1983. This book in the publisher's Literature and Life series tells Rachel Carson's life story.

Sally Lee, *Pesticides.* New York: Franklin Watts, 1991. Discusses the uses of pesticides, the dangers they may pose to our food supply, and governmental restrictions imposed on those considered harmful.

Gino J. Marco, Robert M. Hollingworth, and William Durham, eds., *Silent Spring Revisited.* Washington, DC: American Chemical Society, 1987. This book is based on a symposium held in Philadelphia in August 1984 on the issues raised in *Silent Spring.* It includes a chapter by C.F. Wilkinson, "The Science and Politics of Pesticides."

Periodicals

Brooks Atkinson, "Rachel Carson's Articles on the Danger of Chemical Sprays Prove Effective," *New York Times,* September 11, 1962. This article describes the *New Yorker*'s condensation of *Silent Spring* and identifies the forthcoming book as a case for ecology and mankind, made by stating alarming facts soberly.

R.L. Carson, "Undersea," *Atlantic Monthly*, September 1937. This article, which showcased Carson's beautiful poetic language in a prestigious magazine, started her book-writing career by attracting an offer from Simon & Schuster.

Rachel Carson, "How About Citizenship Papers for the Starling?" *Nature*, June/July 1939. This essay describes how the imported European bird with its voracious appetite saves crops from destructive insects.

Austin H. Clark, "From the Beginning of the World," *Saturday Review of Literature*, July 7, 1951. *The Sea Around Us* is reviewed in a complimentary tone, suggesting that all questions about the ocean are answered in this book.

Edwin Diamond, "The Myth of the Pesticide Menace," *Saturday Evening Post*, September 28, 1963. The author, a scientist, who ended his collaboration with Carson on *Silent Spring*, accuses her of using despicable tactics to scare Americans into believing that their world is being poisoned.

Loren Eiseley, "Using a Plague to Fight a Plague," *Saturday Review*, September 29, 1962. A discussion of chemical pest-killers and how they threaten the existence of birds, fish, farm animals, and ultimately humans.

Martha Freeman, "Rachel's Voice," *Maine Times*, June 1989. The author, a granddaughter of Stanley and Dorothy Freeman, remembers her summer days with Rachel Carson and Roger Christie in Maine and tells how Carson's spirit has influenced her life.

Marjorie Hunter, "U.S. Sets Up Panel to Review the Side Effects of Pesticides," *New York Times*, August 31, 1962. This article reveals that the publication of *Silent Spring* resulted in the formation of a special federal committee to study the effectiveness of government programs dealing with use and control of pesticides.

John M. Lee, "'Silent Spring' Is Now Noisy Summer," *New York Times*, July 22, 1962. Details responses by agricultural chemists to Rachel's book.

Life, "Gentle Storm Center: Calm Appraisal of *Silent Spring*," October 12, 1962. An interview with Carson shows her strong, calm nature and demonstrates how her interests in biology and writing were combined to make her a best-selling author.

New York Times, "Rachel Carson Book Is Called One-Sided," September 14, 1962. This news story reports how the head of the Nutrition Foundation accused Carson of focusing extensively on tragedies of pesticides instead of the positives of maintaining an adequate food supply.

Walter Sullivan, "Books of the Times," *New York Times*, September 27, 1962. The book *Silent Spring* is compared to *Uncle Tom's Cabin*, and its capacity to scare people is considered.

Walter Sullivan, "Chemists Debate Pesticides Book," *New York Times*, September 13, 1962. The *Times* records the belief of chemical industry representatives that *Silent Spring* might slacken the pace of pesticide development.

Stewart L. Udall, "The Legacy of Rachel Carson," *Saturday Review*, May 16, 1964. The author, who was then secretary of the interior, credits Carson with alerting the public to subtle dangers of poisons and the importance of long-term needs of future generations.

Additional Works Consulted

American Forests, "Miss Carson Goes to Congress," July 1963.

Cleveland Amory, "Celebrity Register," *McCall's*, March 1963.

Audubon Magazine, "Rachel Carson Receives Audubon Medal," May 1964.

Shirley A. Briggs, "Silent Spring: The View from 1990," *The Ecologist*, March/April 1990.

Carl W. Buchheister, "The Rachel Carson Memorial Fund for Research," *Audubon Magazine*, July 1964.

Rachel Carson, "A Reporter at Large," *The New Yorker*, June 16, 1962; June 23, 1962; June 30, 1962.

Rachel Carson, "Rachel Carson Answers Her Critics," *Audubon Magazine*, September 1963.

Samuel Epstein and Shirley A. Briggs, "If Rachel Carson Were Writing Today," *Environmental Law Reporter*, June 1987.

Paul Goodman, "Debating Use of Pesticides," *New York Times*, September 21, 1962.

S. Carl Hirsch, *Guardians of Tomorrow, Pioneers in Ecology*. New York: Viking Press, 1971.

Tony Knight, "Public Health Officials to Deploy Predator Fish," *San Fernando Valley Daily News*, March 5, 1993.

Life, "People," February 11, 1952.

New York Times, "Monsanto Dissects Pesticide Criticism," September 22, 1962.

New York Times, "Rachel Carson Dies of Cancer; *Silent Spring* Author Was 56," April 15, 1964.

New York Times, "University Women Give Award to Rachel Carson," June 23, 1956.

New York Times, "Yale Is Bequeathed Rachel Carson Mss," July 20, 1964.

Outdoor Life, "Rachel Carson—A Solitary Crusade for the Outdoors," January 1993.

Pesticide Safety: Myths & Facts. Washington, DC: National Coalition Against the Misuse of Pesticides (pamphlet), 1993.

Publishers' Weekly, "Obituary Notes," April 27, 1964.

Paul Raeburn, "New Research Links DDT, High Breast Cancer Risk," *San Fernando Valley Daily News*, L.A. Life, April 21, 1993.

Saturday Review, "Patroness of Birdsong: Miss Rachel Carson," June 1, 1963.

Jim Tranquada, "Fruit Trees Stripped, Sterile Insects Freed," *San Fernando Valley Daily News*, July 28, 1993.

Mark Wheeler, "Fly Wars," *Discover*, February 1993.

Other Resources

The American Experience, "Rachel Carson's Silent Spring," Public Broadcast System Television, February 8, 1993.

The Beinecke Rare Book and Manuscript Library, Yale University, New Haven, CT, Rachel Carson Papers/Letters.

Paul Brooks, letter to the author, Judith Presnall, September 1, 1993.

Frontline, "In Our Children's Food," Public Broadcast System Television, Spring 1993.

Rachel Carson Council, Inc., 8940 Jones Mill Road, Chevy Chase, MD 20815.

Rachel Carson Homestead Association, 615 Marion Avenue, Springdale, PA 15144.

Rachel Carson National Wildlife Refuge, RR2, Box 751, Route 9 East, Wells, ME 04090.

Index

Picture Credits

Cover photo: © Erich Hartmann/Magnum Photos, Inc.

AP/Wide World, 9, 46, 68, 70, 74, 77

The Beinecke Library, Yale University, 11, 12 (top), 14, 18, 27, 29

From UNDER THE SEA WIND by Rachel L. Carson, illustrated by Bob Hines. Copyright 1941 by Rachel L. Carson. Copyright renewed ©1969 by Roger Christie. Illustrations copyright © 1991 by Bob Hines. A Truman Talley Book. Used by permission of Dutton Signet, a division of Penguin Books USA Inc., 33

CBS Photo—Warnecke, 76

Chatham College, Pittsburgh, PA, 19, 21

Myung J. Chun/*Los Angeles Daily News*, 83 (both)

The Ferdinand Hamburger Jr. Archives of the Johns Hopkins University, 23, 24

By permission of Stanley L. Freeman, 49, 51, 79

© 1988 David Hall/Photo Researchers, Inc., 31, 44

© Erich Hartmann/Magnum Photos, Inc., 50, 52, 56, 62, 63, 66, 78

© 1989 Harold Hoffman/Photo Researchers, Inc., 30

Interior—U.S. Fish and Wildlife Service, 43, 53

©Tom McHugh/George Galicz/Photo Researchers, Inc., 82

Lance O. Presnall, 12 (bottom), 84 (both)

Rachel Carson History Project, 13, 26, 38, 39, 40, 41, 48

University of Minnesota, Minnesota Extension Service, 60

UPI/Bettmann, 9, 36, 54, 58

USDA/APHIS, 57

Woods Hole Oceanographic Institution, 22

About the Author

As part of her research for *The Importance of Rachel Carson*, Judith Janda Presnall traveled to the eastern part of the United States. She visited Rachel's childhood home in Springdale, the windy village called Woods Hole, Johns Hopkins University, the summer Southport Island cottage, and the Silver Spring home with its view of the woods from every window. Judy examined family letters on file at Yale University, visited the Rachel Carson Council, and walked the trail at the Rachel Carson National Wildlife Refuge. She is grateful to her husband, Lance, who accompanied her on the 2,000-mile adventure.

Judy also thanks the following people for sharing information about Rachel Carson: Shirley A. Briggs, Paul Brooks, Martha Freeman, Dr. Diana Post, Nancy Stowers, and Mr. and Mrs. Robert Urick.

Judith Janda Presnall also is the author of award winning *Animals That Glow*. She has received awards from the Society of Children's Book Writers and Illustrators and the California Writers Club. She graduated from the University of Wisconsin, Whitewater, with a degree in education and has taught business classes in high schools and colleges. She lives with her husband, son, Kory, and two cats in the San Fernando Valley in southern California. The Presnalls also have a daughter, Kaye.